30 Classic Mexican Menus

by Idella Purnell Stone

Gramercy Publishing Company
New York

DEDICATED WITH LOVE

to all the good Mexican and American friends who have given me recipes during the last half century, particularly Doña Mercedes Landero de Ayala, who began my Mexican cookbook collection; Luz Landero de Ayala and María Ayala de Zúñiga, for recipes; and María Zúñiga de Ayala, Berta López de González, Helen Balandrán de Ceniceros, and Carrie Purnell de Ceniceros, who helped.

This edition was previously published as part of *30 Classic Mexican Menus in Spanish and English*.

Copyright © 1978 by Idella Purnell Stone

This edition is published by Gramercy Publishing Company, distributed by Crown Publishers, Inc.
h g f e d c b a
GRAMERCY 1981 EDITION

Manufactured in the United States of America

Library of Congress Cataloging in Publication Data

Stone, Idella Purnell, 1901–
    30 classic Mexican menus.

    "Previously published as part of 30 classic Mexican
menus in Spanish and English"—Verso t.p.
    1. Cookery, Mexican. I. Title.
TX716.M4S73   1981   641.5972   81-6256
ISBN 0-517-34744-X   AACR2

Contents

Contents (continued)

Preface

UNTIL ABOUT fifteen years ago Mexican cooking was impracticable in the United States except in the Western States. Even in these it was difficult to find many of the necessary ingredients except in Mexican grocery stores. Now in most cities and many small towns one may find authentic Mexican ingredients or acceptable substitutes.

In Western States, roadsides enlivened by many taco-dispensaries have won acceptance for the simple Mexican equivalent to our own hamburger sandwich. But alas, they have stereotyped the Western American image of Mexican cooking, providing a fixed concept of the taco. It is as though in other lands all the native-born were exposed only to ham sandwiches, with no chance ever to know that here other varieties exist! In Mexico a taco is *anything* wrapped in a tortilla—fried or not—as with us a sandwich is *anything* between two slices of bread.

The relatively few Americans to sample Mexican home cooking or to investigate the cooking of Mexico in depth know that while Mexicans enjoy their chiles and spices, these are only one phase of their cuisine. At home the people enjoy a cooking art that is varied and sophisticated.

The main streams of Mexican culinary arts are Spanish, Moorish, and Mexican Indian: Nahuatl, Zapotecan, Maya, etc. When Mexico was conquered by the Spanish the indigenous population lived largely on maize products and venison, turkey, chiles, tomatoes and onions. They drank thick chocolate seasoned with cinnamon, and octli (pulque) a fermented drink from the heart of the maguey plant. The Aztecs had tamales and tortillas; they roasted their meat in pits and seasoned them with chile sauces.

With the Spaniards came olive oil, garbanzos, codfish, olives and almonds, favorite ingredients in Mexican dishes to this day. They also brought some of their inheritance from the long Moorish occupation of Spain: sweets heavy with honey, pine nuts and rose petals, flavorings of orange flower and rose waters. And they brought the *pastas* of their Italian neighbors, to whom probably Marco Polo introduced them on his return from the fabled long trip to the Orient.

Because the demand for Mexican foods constantly grows, because returned travelers as well as Americans residing in Mexico learn more and more to enjoy these foods, because a complete Mexican meal is a delightful way to entertain friends, and because the ingredients are no longer too difficult to obtain, I give you these *30 Mexican Menus.* I have found that Mexican meals, in addition to satisfying both gourmet and gourmand, are always lively with conversation, and although people may sit down to them as strangers, they rise as friends!

A cookbook is usually easier to use if it provides some guidelines. Here are guidelines for this one.

1. Always read the recipe through before you use it—even though you made it only a week or so before. Sometimes an ingredient is *not* on hand, and this is frustrating.

2. For baking, *always* bring shortening, milk, and eggs from the refrigerator an hour or two before you start; room temperature yields better results. The rule is good for any recipe requiring beaten eggs.

3. Assemble *all* the ingredients. This helps you not to forget anything crucial, such as baking powder.

4. A blender is almost imperative for many of these recipes. If you do not have one, grind nuts in whatever equipment you may have for grinding grains. Many of the sauces are based on a tomato and onion mixture blenderized either before or after cooking. If you lack a blender, cook ingredients until tender, about ten minutes, and press through a sieve with a spoon. Spices may be fresh ground in a Molinex, or a mortar, or a shallow bowl with the bottom of a spoon.

5. I was told by a cook I respected that garlic and salt should *always* be ground together; that this prevents the garlic from "repeating." Therefore I ask you to grind them together. But if you prefer to drop them in the blender with everything else, go ahead.

6. Chiles vary so widely and wildly and come in so many varieties that they are impossible to define accurately. What is hot for one person is medium hot for another and insipid for a third. The easiest way is to buy already prepared Ortega green

6

chiles canned whole or diced. They are precooked. Therefore they are not *quite* the thing to use for uncooked green chile sauce, but with everything else uncooked I don't hesitate to reach for a can of chopped Ortega chiles. If you want them *un*hot (taste, not temp.), search for and discard their seeds. Where chile sauces for enchiladas are required, Las Palmas and La Victoria enchilada sauces are good. Taste them, and if not hot enough, add chile powders. Hot chile powders are: Cayenne, New Mexico, in plastic bags at supermarkets. Medium hot, Gebhardt's. Mild, to add color, more than taste: paprika. Service Foods, Inc., also offers plastic bags of California chile, chile mix for chile con carne, and pasilla chile for other sauces. The very special chile sauce called mole (pronounced mó-leh, and *not* as nationally advertised mo-láy) may be obtained dehydrated in small cans with directions for making, and is satisfactory, although for a turkey two cans or more are needed. I usually add half a cake of bitter chocolate, melted, and more hot chile to this powder. Delicious mole, fully prepared except for thinning to gravy consistency with hot chicken or turkey broth, may be bought in glass containers (La Victoria).

7. Except for desserts and baked goods, most Mexican recipes are quite flexible—i.e., if you don't like garlic it may be omitted, or you may add more tomato or onion than called for—and so on. Most recipes good for one vegetable are equally good for many others. White cheese is used in Mexico for cooking (except in tourist hotels) but you may substitute yellow.

8. Cinnamon is often used in stick form, slivered. Wrap a piece of stick cinnamon in a corner of your kitchen towel and whack it with a hammer. Warn your guests about the slivers— they are edible. One of my guests once began picking the slivers from a tamale—probably thinking they were slivers of wood, and I the world's worst housekeeper.

9. A can of evaporated milk left four to six hours in the refrigerator makes a lovely "whipped cream." However, it falls easily, so should be made just before serving.

In Mexico, whenever one leaves the table ahead of the rest, he wishes them—and they him—*"buen provecho."* Loosely translated, this is "May it do you much good," referring of course to the food and drink. So now, as I take my leave as preface maker, I bow and wish you

BUEN PROVECHO

Menu 1

In the old days of Mexico, the well-to-do often ate two breakfasts: the first desayuno, literally translated break-fast, consisted of a cup of coffee or two with milk and sugar and pan dulce. This sweet Mexican bread makes a delightful coffee cake, especially if one wants to "dunk"—which is perfectly permissible in Mexico. Having broken fast, the city dweller might then rise to go to early Mass—or might turn over and sleep another hour or two. But out on the haciendas the men rose usually at cock crow, prayed in the family chapel, broke their fast, then rode horseback for several hours overseeing the work of the hacienda. They then returned to the big house for their breakfast, called almuerzo, a hearty sort of midmorning lunch, at about 9 or 10. This meal might be coffee, a fruit, a tortilla dish, eggs, sausage, or some other meat—all of them. As the world more and more adopts common customs, the two meals have tended to merge and pattern after the somewhat stereotyped breakfasts of bacon, eggs, toast, marmalade, orange juice, coffee. This is the breakfast served on most Mexican air lines and trains.

You may find it fun to surprise guests with a Mexican breakfast. Here are three.

DESAYUNO

Black coffee extract   Hot milk

Pan dulce

Black coffee extract has appeared in some markets, commercially prepared. If you wish to make your own, buy coffee beans (to be found in large central markets). Toast them until almost black, and grind fine in a coffee mill or blender. Use 1 cupful of powder to 4 cups of water, and boil down to 2 cups. Strain through a fine sieve lined with filter paper, cool, bottle and refrigerate. Remove an hour or two before serving. The cup is first filled with hot milk, sugar to taste, and then coffee extract as desired. A faster extract may be made by adding 1/2 cup instant coffee to 2 cups of boiling water. Bottle and cool. Refrigerate. Remove two hours before serving to warm to room temperature. If you want a real imitation of Mexican coffee extract, select the strongest and blackest instant coffee you can find.

PAN DULCE

Since in Mexico there are many choices of *pan dulce*, here are two recipes. You may like to make and freeze both to have available for your Mexican *desayunos*. They freeze beautifully.

BREAD SPONGE:	*Remaining ingredients:*
2 t. sugar	3/4 c. sugar
3/4 c. lukewarm water	1 T. shortening, melted
1 yeast cake	2 eggs, room temperature,
1 c. sifted flour	beaten
1/4 t. salt	3 c. flour, sifted
	1 to 2 c. flour, sifted

Method: In a medium-sized bowl dissolve sugar in lukewarm water, add yeast cake, crumbled, and stir until completely dissolved. Add the flour and salt and beat well. Cover the bowl with a cloth and stand it in a warm place (not hot), to rise until double in bulk, about an hour. In large mixer bowl cream the sugar and shortening and add the well-beaten eggs; then gradually add two cups of flour, until thoroughly mixed. Add the third cupful to the bread sponge, and mix well. Add the sponge to the

9

mix in large bowl and beat and stir together with a large spoon. Cover with a cloth and again place in warm spot to rise until double, about an hour. Do not let stand too long; it becomes bitter. Now put 1-1/2 cups of flower in sifter, although you may not need it all. Flour bread board (or table top) and turn dough out on it. With a quite moist dough, such as this, it is better first to turn it with a spatula. Fold over the dough and sift some flour over it, folding over again with spatula, and continue flouring and folding until more easily handled. Then with floured hands knead thoroughly. To knead, lift the edge of dough farthest from you, fold it to meet the edge nearest you, press down with heels of your hands to weld the edges together, flip dough around so that an unwelded edge becomes bottom edge and knead and punch together, stretch out and continue kneading and punching and folding until dough becomes elastic and silky and no longer sticks to hands or board—incorporating more flour and flouring board as necessary. This takes 5 to 7 minutes. Shape into half-round ball, flat side down. With sharp knife, slice it through once, then directly across first slice, slice again, to make four pieces. Divide these lengthwise, to make eight; then divide the eight to make 16. Using flour on your hands, quickly dip each cut edge into flour on the board, and shape each segment into a round bun. Have two cookie sheets ready. As each bun is shaped, flour its bottom thoroughly and place it on cookie sheet. Leave plenty of space between buns, and arrange 8 to each sheet. Top with Pan Dulce topping (recipe follows). Cover with a cloth and let rise again in warm place until double in bulk, one hour. Bake at 400° until nicely browned on top, approx. 20 minutes. These burn easily, so watch them during last five minutes. When done, turn oven off and let them cool in the oven. Including rising time: 4 hours. Makes 16.

PAN DULCE TOPPING

1/4 c. shortening	1 t. cinnamon
1/4 c. sugar	3/4 c. flour
1/4 t. salt	

Method: Cream together shortening, sugar, salt, cinnamon. Add the flour and mix until crumbly. Mixture may be sprinkled over the whole bun, and left rough. If you like this easiest method, first brush milk lightly across the bun to make the topping adhere. Another way: With a sharp knife, slash across the bun to make a slight indentation, and move knife to open it a little—about 1/2 inch deep. Take a tablespoonful of topping in palm of hand and squeeze it tightly. This should give it a nice shape, plump in the middle and tapered at each end. Press into the indentation. Cinnamon may be omitted.

PAN DE ADRIANA

4 c. flour
3/4 c. sugar
1 c. milk (room temperature)
1/2 yeast cake or 1/2 pkg.
  dry yeast
1/2 c. ground almonds

4 eggs (room temperature)
1 t. anise
1 c. lard or butter at room
  temperature
1 c. flour

Method: Sift flour and sugar into a large mixing bowl. Heat milk to lukewarm and dissolve the yeast in it. Stir into flour and sugar. Add almonds, eggs and anise, and beat well with a large spoon. This is too stiff for the mixer. When well blended, add softened shortening and continue blending with your hand. Squeeze and press together until smooth and even. Place flour in sifter and sift half of it onto bread board. Spread it and empty dough onto flour. Knead and thump and lift dough as described in *Pan Dulce* recipe, until none sticks to board or hands, and most of the flour, or all, has been used. Butter two loaf pans (9"x5"x3"). Divide dough into two equal parts and shape two loaves. Place in pans and set in a warm place to rise, covered with cloth. Let rise until double, 3-1/2 to 4 hours. Bake in 350° oven 50 to 60 minutes. This attractive golden bread is delicious, served hot or cold. Two loaves. Time, including 3-1/2 hour rising time: 4-3/4 hours.

Menu 2

ALMUERZO

This is a hearty breakfast and is designed to keep the consumer going until the 2:30 dinnertime.

Papaya with Lemon Wedges	Eggs with Chorizo
Gorditas	Coffee

PAPAYA WITH LEMON WEDGES

Cut papaya through lengthwise. Remove and discard black pep-percorn-like seeds. Serve each papaya half on a small attractive plate with one or two lemon wedges (but please, no paprika.) Papaya is lovely alone, or with lemon juice, or with salt, or with salt and lemon.

EGGS WITH CHORIZO

Chorizo is Mexican sausage, seasoned heavily with garlic, oré-gano and chile. Polish kohlbase, Italian anise sausage, make good substitutes. Our own sausage doesn't because sage is not a Mexican seasoning. It is easy to make your own chorizo, and good to have some on hand for other recipes in this book.

CHORIZO

1 lb. ground beef	1 t. coriander, ground
1 lb. ground pork (unseasoned)	1 t. cumin, ground
	1-1/2 t. cayenne pepper (fiery)
3 cloves garlic crushed with 1 t. salt	1 t. pepper
	1 t. salt
1/2 t. orégano, finely crushed	1/2 c. vinegar
1-3 t. New Mexico chile powder (very hot)	1/2 c. sherry

Method: Place the meats in a large bowl. Grind the garlic and salt in a mortar, add the orégano and seeds and spices, and blend with the garlic. Work in the additional teaspoonful of salt. Add the vinegar and sherry and stir until well blended. Pour all this

12

over the meats and work it in with your hand to mix thoroughly. Be sure to mix *very* thoroughly, because the vinegar and sherry "cure" the meat and prevent spoilage. Cover with cloth and stand bowl in a cool place until the next day. Divide into serving portions and shape them like fat weiners. Wrap each in a piece of saran wrap. Freeze all you do not plan to use soon. Store the rest in a covered jar in your refrigerator. Let season for at least three days before using. Time: 20-25 minutes. Two pint jars—if packed solid without shaping.

EGGS WITH CHORIZO

4 links chorizo, or 1 cupful if   1 T. cooking oil
   homemade   8 eggs

Method: Peel chorizo. In a large pan heat just enough oil to prevent sticking. Fry the chorizo, crumbling it with fork as it fries until it is well-browned, about 10 minutes. If it has released too much fat, reduce to 2-3 tablespoonsful. Break eggs into a bowl, beat slightly with a fork, pour into the chorizo and continue cooking and stirring over medium heat until scrambled to desired consistency. (7-10 min.) These are excellent with hot tortillas or with gorditas. Time: 20 min. Serves 4-6.

GORDITAS

2 c. Masa Harina   1 t. salt
2 T. melted shortening or   1-1/2 c. boiling water
   cooking oil   Cooking oil for frying

Method: Most supermarkets now carry Masa Harina, the dehydrated *masa*. Thoroughly mix the Masa Harina, oil, salt, and boiling water. If not rushed, let dough stand for 10 to 20 minutes, to firm. Shape into round, patty-like cakes, the size of uncooked biscuits. Heat 1/2 inch of shortening in a large pan and fry them until golden brown on both sides, about 3-4 minutes to a side. Use a pancake turner. Time, without standing: approx. 20 min. Makes 16.

Menu 3

Orange Juice   Huevos Rancheros
    Frijoles   Tortillas
              Coffee

HOT CHILE SAUCE

Here are some good quick hot chile sauces—and if your friends gasp and call for glasses of cold water, remember that cold milk is really much better than cold water for moderating the flames!

Chiles (red, green, yellow)
   1/2 to 1 c.
1 c. tomatillos
1-2 cloves of garlic
1 to 1-1/2 t. salt

Cilantro (Chinese parsley;
   coriander herb) to taste
   (optional)
Limewater (optional)

Method: For this recipe, use fresh chiles, red for red sauce, green for chile verde sauce. Tomatillos may be obtained canned at Mexican markets and at supermarkets. Grind together in your blender the drained tomatillos with chiles, first removing the chiles' stems, seeds, and inside white membranes. Add a clove or two of garlic—if you wish. Add salt to taste. If you can find cilantro, add that too, discarding tough stems, until its flavor is noticeable. For a truly hot sauce I would use a cupful of chiles for each cup of tomatillos; but to each his own: use only a few chiles to begin, taste, and add more as you may wish. If you make the sauce extremely hot, a tablespoonful or two of lime water helps counteract the effect on the stomach lining. To make this, buy hydrated lime at drug store (expensive) or plant nursery (cheap). Fill a gallon jug with clear pure water (we hope) add a large tablespoonful of the lime, and let settle a few days before using.

RED CHILE SAUCE

2-6 red chiles
2 large tomatoes
1/2 large onion, minced
1-2 cloves garlic

1 to 1-1/2 t. salt
1/4 to 1/2 t. orégano
1 T. lime water

14

Red chile sauce is as easily made, and is more often used with eggs. Remove chiles' stems, seeds, and inside white membranes. Grind the chiles with one or two large tomatoes, add half an onion finely chopped, garlic if wanted, and salt. Add a pinch of orégano and a tablespoonful of lime water. The quantity of each ingredient is best determined, as with the green sauce, by the cook. Roughly speaking, use half a cupful of red chiles to two large tomatoes—and you will soon know if you prefer more or less chile.

Either of these raw chile sauces is excellent for Huevos Rancheros. A third sauce, used almost as often, is cooked:

Cooked Chile Sauce: Make the red chile sauce. Heat two tablespoonsful of cooking oil, pour the red sauce into it, and simmer ten minutes. Use hot over the eggs. The other two sauces are used, cold, and the contrast of cold sauce with hot egg is rather pleasant. Of course the easiest way is to buy a bottle of either red or green chile sauce at your supermarket, and heat the sauce or pour it over the eggs straight from the bottle, as you wish.

HUEVOS RANCHEROS

4 T. cooking oil	8 eggs
1 c. red or green chile sauce, warmed	Salt

Method: In a large pan, heat cooking oil. In a smaller pan, heat chile sauce. When the oil is hot, break each egg into a saucer and slide it from saucer into hot oil, reducing heat to keep from burning. Fry until whites are well set (hasten this by spooning fat over them.) Remove eggs to warmed deep plates, and pour one or two tablespoonsful of sauce over each. If you wish, pass additional heated sauce. Serve with plenty of hot tortillas. If you use cold sauce, it should be at room temperature, not refrigerator cold, or it will chill the eggs. Serves 4. Time: Approx. 10 minutes.

TORTILLAS

MY BEST ADVICE ON THESE IS TO BUY THEM MADE IF YOU CAN—unless you have some Mexican genes. The most important rule is: NEVER UNDER ANY CIRCUMSTANCES SERVE COLD TORTILLAS. To refresh tortillas: Heat a large griddle over medium heat. Run tortilla rapidly under hot water from faucet. Shake off excess moisture and place tortilla on griddle. Allow about one minute to each side—only enough to dry and heat the tortilla. Should tortillas begin to stick, very lightly grease griddle. If you cannot find tortillas to buy, you will have to make them—or forego some pleasant Mexican culinary adventures.

CORN TORTILLAS

| 2 c. "masa" | OR | 2 c. Masa Harina |
| | | 1-1/2 c. warm water |

Method: If you can buy your "masa" already made from a tortilla factory in your vicinity, you need nothing else—unless the masa has grown too dry in which case add a little hot water to make it malleable. Otherwise, use Masa Harina. This is dehydrated "masa" made by the Quaker Oats Company, and I am forever grateful to them for thus making my cookbook possible; before the advent of Masa Harina unless you had a source of masa near at hand it was impossible to indulge in making many recipes described in this book. In a medium bowl, place two cupsful of Masa Harina, and pour the warm water into it. Combine well to make a smooth stiff dough. Shape dough into balls the size of a large walnut. (About ten minutes.) Let stand 20 min. if you have time. It makes them less sticky. Wet and wring out thoroughly two non-terry clean dishtowels. (Or substitute waxed paper. I like the cloths.) Spread one on bread board. Place about 3 balls on it, well apart, cover with the second cloth, and roll out as thin as you can without breaking them. It takes practice. Remove to griddle and do the next few. A second method, which I prefer, is to substitute a small smooth board for the rolling pin. Press it down with a firm even pressure on one ball of dough at a time until a perfectly shaped tortilla is formed. Very lightly grease griddle, reduce heat to medium,

16

and bake tortillas on it quickly. When the flat surface of the tortilla balloons up, or begins to blister, turn the tortilla quickly to bake until it balloons or blisters again. About three minutes to each side. Mexican tortilla makers always turn their tortillas with their fingers, so skillfully they never burn them, but for non-Mexican a pancake turner is better. Time (without standing): about 30 min. Makes 12.

FRIJOLES

In the old days in Mexico one could always tell when near the end of the long many-coursed dinner because then the frijoles appeared. They *always* preceded the dessert. They came with delicate fresh hot tortillas, or *birotes*, a Mexican bread, very like French bread, probably introduced during Maximilian's brief and tragic reign.

Mexican-cooked frijoles seldom cause indigestion or gas; the secret probably is their cooking method. The University of New Mexico did prolonged researches into frijol cooking methods, and ended by recommending the Mexican way as best. Use pink or pinto beans. They usually come now pot-ready; if they aren't, pick them over carefully and wash well. Place in a large pot with cold *soft* water to cover deeply (rain water is perfect) bring quickly to a boil, reduce heat to medium or below and simmer, not too slowly—three to four hours, until the beans are tender. *Do not salt* until the beans are thoroughly tender. Test by occasionally taking out a bean and crushing it between your fingers. When the bean crushes easily, eat one! When *truly* done, the bean loses its rawness and tastes good. Now salt them. But if it is still hours before dinner, reduce the heat more and let them go on cooking. The longer they cook the better they are, and the longer you can put off the salting, which toughens the skin. Allow 6 to 8 cups of water for each cupful of beans. Should they begin to appear above the level of water in pot, add boiling water.

Mexicans often serve *"frijoles de la olla,"* which means "beans fresh from the pot," and they are excellent. The method: Crush well or blenderize a cupful of cooked beans, return to pot—and serve. With fresh tomatoes, little green onions, lettuce and good cheese, preferably a white variety, these make a delicious supper;

17

and with either a fresh uncooked or bottled green or red chile sauce, a pleasing spiciness may be added.

More often frijoles are served *fritos* (fried) and *refritos* (refried). *Method:* After beans are cooked and salted, in a large pan heat about 1/2 cup cooking oil until hot. Ladle beans into the fat (about a cupful at a time) and crush them well with a large long-handled spoon, or potato masher. As soon as a cupful has blended with the oil, add a second cupful; and if the mixture thickens too much, some liquid from the pot, and crush again. If you need more than four cupfuls of beans, add more oil—about 1/4 cupful for every two cups of beans. The consistency should be much like that of mashed potatoes, fluffy and soft. For *frijoles refritos*, heat cooking oil in a large pan and in it fry yesterday's frijoles fritos, when any are left over. If quantity isn't enough, add some more beans from pot, and crush them. Otherwise, as they are already crushed, you stir them until all the oil is worked into them, and let them repose there only long enough to make a slightly crusty bottom; fold over with pancake turner *a la* omelet, and sprinkle with grated dry white cheese, Romano or Parmesan. . . .

The easiest way, of course, is to buy a large can of *Rosarita Refried Beans*, and then refry them! The commercial beans sometimes are less carefully crushed than the home cook's, so after adding them to the hot oil, with a long strong spoon find and mash any whole beans—or use your potato masher.

It makes me sad to think that frijoles and tortillas are not as much used in Mexico as formerly, above all when I recall that frijoles are full of iron and tortillas of calcium, and that from them the Mexicans have derived their strong skeletons and beautiful firm teeth. Now that we all need more health-giving and vital elements, we should enjoy more, not less, tortillas and frijoles.

Frijoles fritos: time, not counting boiling time: 4 cups, about ten minutes. Refried: about four minutes. Serves 8. The canned Rosarita Refried Beans serve 7 4-oz. portions.

18

Menu 4

Avocado Soup   Kidneys in Wine
Vegetable Soufflé   Orange Baskets

AVOCADO SOUP

4 tortillas
4 T. cooking oil
4 avocados, finely cubed
1/2 bunch watercress, 1 inch
  lengths
1 brown onion, minced

1-1/2 c. tomatoes, cubed (or
  canned, well crushed)
6 c. beef broth or consommé
  (or use 6 c. boiling water
  and 6 chicken or beef
  bouillon cubes)

Method: Slice tortillas once across middle, then stack and cut in
1/2 inch strips. Heat two tablespoonsful cooking oil. In this fry
the tortillas until golden brown over medium heat. (About 5
min.) Keep them warm. Peel and cube avocados. Discard hard
stems of cress and cut the cress into 1 inch lengths. Heat remaining oil, buzz onion and tomato in blender and pour into hot oil.
Reduce heat and simmer mixture until thick (10 min.). Heat
beef broth in large saucepan. Pour tomato mixture into heated
broth; add salt and pepper to taste. Boil rapidly 15 minutes.
Place tortillas, avocados and cress in a large tureen; pour boiling
broth over them and serve at once. Total time: 40 min. Serves 8.

KIDNEYS IN WINE

1 lb. beef kidneys
2 lemons
2 T. cooking fat
1 large onion, minced
2 c. tomato pulp

1 t. finely minced parsley
3 T. green olive bits
1/4 t. pepper
1 t. salt
1/4 c. sherry

Method: Wash kidneys. Remove fat. Slice kidneys thin and pour
the juice of two lemons over them. Stir well. Let stand one hour
at room temperature. Drain and dry with paper towels. In large
pan, heat the cooking oil, add the onions and cook until transparent, 3-5 minutes. Add kidneys, stir and turn until browned.

Cover and reduce heat. Buzz tomatoes in blender and add with the parsley and olives to the kidneys. Simmer until thick, about 10 minutes. Add sherry, stir again, cover and simmer three minutes more. Serve at once. Total time: 1-1/2 hours. Serves 4.

VEGETABLE SOUFFLE

2 medium-sized carrots	5 eggs
1 small turnip	3 T. flour
2 medium-sized zucchini	3 T. Cheddar cheese, grated
3-4 cauliflower florets	1/2 c. cream
1 c. peas	3 T. bread crumbs

Method: Preheat oven to 350°. Slice vegetables very thin. Florets should be about 1/2 cup. Peas may be canned. Cook the vegetables (except peas) together in 1/2 cup water, with tight lid on utensil so that they steam more than boil. At end of 15 minutes, add fresh peas. If peas are canned, drain them. At end of 5 more minutes, drain vegetables thoroughly; reserve water to make soup. While draining, separate whites of eggs into large mixer bowl, yolks into smaller one. Beat whites very stiff. Beat yolks stiff, and still beating, add flour, cheese, and cream. Mix all vegetables into the yolk mixture. Liberally butter a two quart casserole; press crumbs firmly into the butter. Combine yolk mixture with whites, pour into casserole, and bake, uncovered, in a large pan with water in it, for an hour. Serve in the casserole. Time: 1-1/2 hours. Serves 6-8.

ORANGE BASKETS

6 large oranges	1 c. whipping or all purpose cream
2 slices canned pineapple	
2 ripe bananas	1 T. powdered sugar
1/2 c. sugar	1/2 t. almond extract
1/2 c. strawberries, sliced	6 large strawberries

Method: Fine big navel oranges are the best for this recipe; others will do. Wash oranges thoroughly in hot soapy water and then in cold to remove any traces of sprays, unless you *know* they are from unsprayed trees. Dry well. Cut a round segment

20

off the bottom. Excavate all the pulp you can, using potato peeler, small sharp knife, and spoon; discard white membranes. Clean out shell. Place pulp in a mixing bowl and combine with the sliced pineapple and bananas and sugar. Gently fold in sliced strawberries, avoiding crushing them. Fill the rinds with this mixture. Whip the cream, add powdered sugar and almond extract a second or two before beating ends. If desired, tint this cream pale pink with vegetable coloring. Heap the orange baskets, with spoon or decorating tube. In center of each place one whole strawberry. Refrigerate two hours. Time (less refrigeration) 35 min. Serves 6.

If you don't want to bother with baskets, make the fruit mixture and serve it in small attractive bowls, or on a large platter, decorated with the cream and strawberries.

Menu 5

Vegetable Soup
Corn Patties

Beef and Potatoes
Chocolate Flan

VEGETABLE SOUP

2 T. cooking oil
1-1/2 c. tomato pulp
1 large brown onion, minced
8 c. beef broth (save from
    recipe below, or use
    bouillon cubes)
3 turnips, cubed

3 carrots, sliced thin across
1/2 c. peas
1 c. string beans, 1 in.
    lengths, *or* 1/2 pkg. frozen
    string beans, French style
2 T. tapioca

Method: Heat oil, add tomato pulp and onion buzzed together in
blender; simmer until thick, about 10 minutes. Add to the
beef broth with all the vegetables. Season to taste with salt and
pepper. If broth is unseasoned, this will take about two t. salt,
1/2 t. pepper. When boiling starts, sprinkle in tapioca gently.
Reduce heat and cook about 1/2 hour more, until vegetables are
tender and tapioca transparent. This one brings requests for
"seconds." Time: 45 min. Serves 8.

BEEF AND POTATOES

10 c. water
3 lbs. top round
3 medium potatoes, boiled,
    peeled, cubed
3 T. cooking fat
1 slice of bread
1/2 c. peanuts without skins
    (or 4 T. peanut butter)

1 clove garlic, finely minced
1 large onion, finely minced
2 c. tomato pulp
3 whole cloves
1 t. cinnamon
2 t. salt
1/2 t. pepper

Method: In a five quart pot bring water to a rapid boil and
plunge in the meat, add the washed unpeeled potatoes. Reduce
heat and simmer gently until beef is tender, about two hours.
When potatoes are done (test with fork) after first 20 min.,
remove them, peel and dice. While meat cooks, heat oil in a

22

small pan. Fry the bread and peanuts until golden, then buzz them in your blender, adding a little broth if necessary, along with the garlic, onion, tomatoes, cloves, cinnamon, pepper and salt. Return to the pan in which the bread and peanuts fried and simmer until thick, about ten minutes. When the meat is tender, remove and slice it. In a large pan place two cups of the broth, add the tomato mixture, the meat slices, and the potatoes. Bring to a rapid boil, cover, reduce heat and simmer an additional ten minutes, or until sauce thickens. Should it be too watery still after fifteen minutes, quickly grind and add another slice of bread, stir well and simmer only long enough to rectify the wateriness—4 or 5 minutes. Approx. 2 hours 20 minutes, including boiling. Serves 8, generously.

CORN PATTIES

Sauce
1 T. cooking oil
1 small green onion,
    sliced thin
2 canned green chiles, minced
1 can tomato soup, undiluted
1/2 lb. fresh cheese (Jack or
    Muenster preferred) finely
    chopped

Patties:
4 ears of tender corn
4 T. sour cream
2 eggs
3 T. flour
1/2 c. cooking oil

Method: Heat cooking oil, add onion. When onion is transparent, add the chiles and soup; stir and simmer 10 min. Keep warm. Prepare cheese, but do not add. To make the patties, clean corn thoroughly and slice from ears. Use potato-peeler; slice half way down the cob very lightly to remove tops of kernels, then again go over it with a heavier stroke until all the grains yield their edible portions—then repeat with the second half. Blenderize corn. Transfer to mixer and beat in the cream, eggs, and flour. Heat the oil and drop the mixture in by tablespoonsful. Brown well on both sides, about 2-3 min. to each side. Place in deep dish to conserve heat. Reheat tomato sauce, add cheese, stir well and pour over the patties. Makes 20. Time: 25 minutes. Serves 8. You may use canned corn, but fresh is better!

CHOCOLATE FLAN

1 oz. (1 square) bitter
  chocolate
1/4 c. water
2 c. evaporated or well-boiled
  milk

6 egg yolks
1 T. vanilla
1 c. sugar

Method: Preheat oven to 350°. Set large pan of water in oven, with mold in pan. I use an oval baking casserole, 1-1/2 quart size. In double boiler top, over hot water, melt chocolate in 1/4 c. water. Add to the milk beaten with the yolks and vanilla and 1/2 c. sugar. Beat well. Caramelize 1/2 c. sugar over high heat in a small saucepan, stirring hard. When sugar begins to melt, reduce heat and continue stirring until sugar has all melted and is a light tan. Do not burn—it turns bitter. Pour it into the bottom of the mold, and tilt to cover all the bottom. Pour the chocolate mixture into the mold. Bake one hour. Cool thoroughly. (Make it the day before use and let it firm in refrigerator.) Slide spatula around upper edge of custard to loosen; place a large platter with some depth over the casserole, and invert carefully. Let mold remain about fifteen minutes so all the caramel sauce can drip down. Preparation time: about 15 min. Serves 6.

QUICKIE VERSION:

1 quart chocolate milk
5 yolks
1 whole egg

1/2 c. sugar
Sugar for caramelizing as
  above

Method: Prepare oven and pan of hot water and caramelize bottom of mold as in prior recipe. In mixer, beat yolks and egg with sugar, add chocolate milk; pour into mold, set in pan of hot water, and bake an hour. This makes a very pretty dish as the chocolate milk tends to divide into two layers, a dark layer and a lighter one, thus looking quite sophisticated! Add vanilla flavoring or not, as desired. Preparation time: about 5 minutes. Serves 6.

Menu 6

Artichoke Soup   Capirotada
Poached Eggs   Acapulco Avocado Salad
                    Pineapple Flan

ARTICHOKE SOUP

8 artichokes or 1 can (14 oz.)   2 T. flour
   artichoke hearts   1 t. salt
1 large onion   1/4 t. pepper
2 quarts milk   2 egg yolks
3 T. butter   1 c. oyster crackers

Method: Wash artichokes thoroughly. Remove and discard outer
leaves. Scrape "choke" from the hearts, cut hearts in halves. Peel
and slice the onion. Buzz hearts and onion with 1/2 cup of milk
in your blender. Heat the butter, add the flour and stir to a
paste; then add the artichoke mixture. Stir until thick, about five
minutes. Heat the rest of the milk and add the artichoke mixture;
stir well, and season with salt and pepper to taste. Lightly beat
the egg yolks and mix a little of the heated soup with them, then
add yolks to the soup. Stir well. Made with fresh artichokes this is
a pleasing light green; but with canned hearts it is an unbecom-
ing grey; add a few drops of green vegetable coloring to correct
this. Serve with oyster crackers sprinkled over the top. Total
time: approx. 25 minutes. Serves 8.

CAPIROTADA

1 loaf French bread (1 lb. —   2 c. sugar
   the long kind, about two   5 cloves
   feet)   1 stick cinnamon (abt. 3 in.)
1/2 c. cooking oil   4-6 tortillas
4 c. water   1/4 c. blanched almonds,
4 large tomatoes, peeled and   halved
   cubed, *or* 1 #2-1/2 can   1/4 c. raisins
   tomatoes   1/2 c. grated dry cheese—
1 large onion, minced   Romano or Parmesan

Method: Cut loaf in half through center lengthwise, between upper and lower crusts. Cut halves into four or five inch sections. In a large pan heat cooking oil and quickly fry top and bottom of bread; try not to burn it. You may need more oil; the bread soaks it up hungrily. Grease a large (17" x 12" x 2-1/2") pan with butter; grease tortillas on *both* sides and cover the bottom of the pan with them (prevents sticking.) Arrange the fried bread in the pan. In two quart pot, bring the water, tomatoes, onion, sugar, cloves, and stick cinnamon well crushed, to a boil. Reduce heat slightly, and boil vigorously until reduced to half, about an hour. Pour syrup over bread in pan, being sure that each piece is well covered, then sprinkle with raisins and almonds and grated cheese. If some of the bread was left, use it for a second layer and repeat the operation. Use all of the syrup and other ingredients. Cover with aluminum foil, and bake in preheated 350° oven 20 minutes; remove foil, and bake 5 minutes more. Total time: approx. 1 hour, 45 min. Serves 10 amply, 12 to 14 adequately.

This may be used as a "sopa seca" or dry soup, following the wet soup. If an entrée, as in this menu, each serving of capirotada is topped with a beautifully poached hot egg, and is considered an adequate meat substitute.

ACAPULCO AVOCADO SALAD

3 T. olive oil
3 T. vinegar
1 t. salt
1/2 t. black pepper
1 t. chile powder
4 green onions, finely sliced

4 medium tomatoes, peeled and diced
2 t. finely minced parsley
4 avocados
1 c. papaya cubes (optional)

Method: Mix oil, vinegar, salt, pepper, chile powder. Cut tomatoes and onions into a bowl and mix well. Add parsley. Halve avocadoes lengthwise and discard seeds. With a spoon carefully remove most of the meat, being careful not to puncture shells; break up large pieces, and toss the avocado with the tomato mix and dressing. If desired, add papaya cubes also. Chill shells and salad. To serve, spoon salad into shells. Not counting refrigeration, total time: 25 min. Serves 8.

PINEAPPLE FLAN

1 c. pineapple juice
1/2 c. sugar
6 eggs

1/4 c. sugar for caramelizing
(optional)

Method Cook the pineapple juice and sugar to a syrup by boiling hard and stirring five minutes. Beat eggs until very light and stiff. Pour two tablespoonsful of the syrup into a one quart baking dish and turn to coat the bottom and sides (or if you wish caramelize the additional sugar and use this instead.) Pour remaining syrup into beaten eggs, and briefly beat again. Pour into baking dish. Set in pan of hot water and bake in pre-heated 350° oven 45 minutes to 1 hour. Cool. Cover and refrigerate. Best when made day before serving. Run knife around edge of flan and unmold on platter to serve. Total time—1 hour. Serves 6.

Menu 7

Foam Soup   Turkey Mole
Turnips with Milk   Old-Fashioned Dessert

FOAM SOUP

1/2 c. butter (1/4 lb.)
1 c. flour
1 t. baking powder
6 t. grated Romano cheese
3 eggs
4 c. chicken or meat broth

1 can tomato soup *or* 1-1/2 c.
tomato juice (depending
on whether you want soup
thick or clear)
1/8 t. orégano
1/4 t. pepper

Method: Melt butter. Blend in flour, baking powder and cheese.
Remove from heat. Beat egg whites until very stiff. Still beating,
add one yolk at a time, being sure each blends in before adding
the next. Still beating slowly, add flour and cheese mixture, a
little at a time. (10 minutes.) Heat the broth and combine
tomato soup (or juice) with it. Add orégano and pepper. When
boiling, drop in egg and cheese mix, a teaspoonful at a time.
Makes 16. (10 minutes.) Cover tightly, reduce heat so mixture
won't boil over, and cook 10 minutes. The dumplings puff into
flavorful balls. Serve in large tureen, as soon as done. Time: 30
min. Serves 8.

TURKEY MOLE

1 turkey, 10-15 lbs.
2 8-1/2 oz. jars La
   Victoria Mole Poblano

CHICKEN MOLE

1 large chicken
1 8-1/2 oz. La Victoria
   Mole Poblano

Method: Boil fowl in water to cover until tender (1 hour for
chicken, 1-1/2 to 2 for turkey), adding a bay leaf, onion, few
cloves of garlic, any or all, as you wish. When fowl is tender,
drain, reserving liquid. When cool enough to handle, debone.
Cut meat in bite sizes. In very large saucepan, empty the mole;
add some of the liquid from pot and stir over medium flame.
Add more liquid as needed until all the sauce is the consistency
of a good thick gravy, neither like library paste, nor runny. Add
meat and about 1/2 cupful of additional broth, stir well and

28

simmer five minutes. Serve with plenty of hot tortillas. Mole sauce also comes in small cans, dehydrated, but is not as good as the moist kind in jars, which is as good as any of the excellent moles I have enjoyed in Mexico . . . with hours less of work and much less expense. Chicken recipe serves approx. 8; turkey recipe, 10-15 . . . more if there is much additional food. Time for sauce: approx. 10 minutes.

TURNIPS WITH MILK

8 medium-sized turnips	1/2 t. salt
1/8 lb. butter (1/2 stick)	1/8 t. freshly ground pepper
2 T. flour	1/2 to 1 t. freshly grated
1 c. milk	nutmeg

Method: Boil turnips until tender. Cooking time depends on size. When fork easily goes into largest turnip, they're done. Peel, slice into cubes about 1/2 inch square. Melt butter over medium heat. Blend in flower, add milk and seasonings, and stir until thick (5 min.) Taste to correct seasoning—you may like more nutmeg, but start with 1/2 teaspoonful. Taste should be noticeable. Add turnips, and serve. Time: 25 min. Serves 8.

OLD-FASHIONED DESSERT

3/4 c. sugar	6-8 cake slices (pound,
1/2 c. water	sponge, any plain cake)
4 whole cloves	5 egg yolks
1/2 c. sherry	

Method: Boil sugar, water and cloves together for five minutes. Cool. Add sherry. While syrup cools, arrange cake slices on a large platter and pour half the sherry-syrup over them. (I like to arrange the slices like petals of a flower on a large round platter, their ends meeting toward the center, leaving a hole about three inches across. Between cake slices long segments of large peaches or nectarines are placed). Now slightly beat yolks, pour a little syrup into them and stir, empty into the remaining syrup and stir over medium heat until mixture coats the spoon. (5 min.) Pour over the cake, making sure each slice gets its share. Garnish as desired. Serve hot or cold. Not including time to make cake, 15 min. Serves 8.

Menu 8

Tongue with Prune Sauce
Carrots in Milk

Potato with Ricotta
Ice Cream with Cajeta

Coffee

TONGUE WITH PRUNE SAUCE

1 large beef tongue
(2-1/2 to 3 lbs.)
2 bay leaves
8 peppercorns
1 t. salt

1 lb. prunes
1 stick cinnamon
1/4 c. sugar
1/4 c. red dry wine
1/2 head lettuce, coarsely sliced

Method: Cover tongue with cold water in a large pot. Add bay leaves, peppercorns and salt. Bring to a boil. Reduce heat and cook, covered, for 2 to 2-1/2 hours—until fork easily penetrates meat at large end. Drain tongue and cool 10 minutes. Reserve liquid for soups. With a sharp knife, remove fat and gristle from large end. Slit skin on bottom of tongue lengthwise. Loosen skin at large end by easing knife under it, and peel it off. The skin removes like a glove when this is done correctly. Discard fat, gristle, bones and skin. Unless you wish to serve it whole, cut in half-inch thick slices. Time: 2-3/4 hours.

Prune sauce: Soak prunes in water to barely cover for an hour. When plump, add cinnamon and sugar, and if needed, more water. Bring to boil. Cover, reduce heat and simmer until prunes are tender and syrup thick, about 20 minutes. Remove, drain, and reserve liquid. Discard cinnamon and prune seeds. Mash pulp. Blend in wine and enough of prune liquid to make sauce the consistency of boiled custard. Or place prunes in blender with wine and buzz, adding prune liquid by tablespoonful until right consistency is reached. With seeded prunes and blender, about 3 minutes. Otherwise, 10. Cut lettuce in half and slice one half in 1/2 inch slices; separate into shreds. Arrange on a large platter. Accommodate whole or sliced tongue on lettuce. Pour prune sauce over tongue, or pass in a gravy-boat to let each serve himself. This is an excellent recipe. If any prune sauce remains, use it as a topping (another day) for ice cream! Total time: 3 hours. Serves 8.

30

POTATOES WITH RICOTTA

6 medium potatoes, peeled
2 T. cooking oil
1 clove garlic, finely minced
1 t. salt

1 can minced green chiles
(Ortega)
1/4 lb. ricotta cheese or
Mexican requesón

Method: Boil potatoes in water to cover until tender, about 20 minutes. Drain well. Slice in thin slices. Peel and finely mince garlic. In a large pan, heat the oil. Add garlic, reduce heat and simmer 3 min. or until garlic is transparent. Add potatoes. Add chiles with their liquid, and salt. Stir well, cover, and simmer for ten minutes. Stir several times to prevent sticking. If very dry, add one or two tablespoons of very hot water. Taste to correct seasoning: you may like more salt. Stir in cheese, remove to serving dish and serve at once. Time: about 40 minutes. Serves 8.

CARROTS COOKED IN MILK

6 to 8 medium carrots
1 c. evaporated milk
1 t. sugar

1/2 t. pepper
1 t. salt
3 T. butter

Method: For fast cooking, select nice tender *young* carrots— crisp ones, with tips that do not bend flexibly. Fresh carrots break. (But careful, don't break them.) Wash but do not peel. Slice very thin in rounds. Grease a quart and a half casserole, place carrot slices in it, cover with milk, add sugar, pepper, salt and butter. If needed, supply a little more milk. Bake covered at 450° until tender, 1/2 hour. Serves 6.

ICE CREAM WITH CAJETA

1 can sweetened condensed
milk
1 small can crushed pineapple

1 qt. vanilla or coffee ice
cream

Method: Place condensed milk, intact—don't even remove label—in water to cover and boil two hours. Be sure to keep can completely covered throughout boiling. Cook completely. Punch hole in one end of can, remove the other end, and slide out into bowl. Drain pineapple and mix with the cajeta. Use as topping for ice cream. Serves 8-10. Very rich!

Menu 9

Potato Soup   Stuffed Zucchini
Meat Rounds   Coconut Sweet

POTATO SOUP

3 large potatoes, peeled and grated
1/4 c. cooking oil
2 c. tomato pulp
1 large onion, minced

2 T. cooking oil
3 c. broth, meat or chicken
1/4 c. grated dry white cheese—Romano or Parmesan

Method: Peel and coarsely grate potatoes, plunge into salted water for ten minutes. Remove and dry with paper towels. Heat 1/4 c. cooking oil and fry the potatoes to golden brown: about ten minutes. Drain excess grease and keep potatoes warm in a large tureen. Blend the tomato and onion. Heat the 2 T. oil and in it simmer the tomato mixture until thick, about ten minutes. Heat broth, add tomato mixture, and boil 15 minutes. Add grated cheese, and pour over the potatoes. Serve at once. Time: 55 minutes. Serves 8.

STUFFED ZUCCHINI

12 tender zucchini
1/2 lb. soft white cheese, Jack, cream or Muenster cut in strips to fit zucchini
2 eggs

1 t. salt
1/2 t. pepper
2 t. flour
Fat for frying

Method: Parboil zucchini in boiling salted water five minutes. Cut in halves, carefully remove centers with spoon, place strips of cheese in halves and fill with zucchini pulp, then fasten each two halves together with toothpicks, to remove before serving. Beat whites of eggs very stiff, still beating add yolks, slowly, one at a time; then salt, pepper, and flour. Heat oil for frying (about 1/2 inch in pan). Dip zucchini in egg batter and fry until well browned on both sides. Time: 20-25 minutes. Serves 4-6.

32

MEAT ROUNDS

1 lb. ground round
2 large potatoes, peeled and
   boiled
1 t. salt
1/2 t. pepper
2 eggs
1/4 c. bread crumbs

1/2 c. cooking oil
1 lettuce, sliced
2 stalks celery, thinly sliced
2 tomatoes, sliced
2 hard-cooked eggs, sliced
   Parsley

Method: Place meat in bowl, mash and add the potatoes, two
T. of crumbs, salt and pepper. Mix well with hand. Shape into
thin patties, about five inches across—makes 8. Beat egg whites
stiff, still beating add yolks, one at a time; remove, and dip patties first into egg batter and then into crumbs. Heat cooking oil
and fry patties until browned on both sides, about 7 minutes to
a side. Slice lettuce and celery and toss with 3 T. olive oil, sprinkle with 2 T. vinegar and toss again. Spread salad mixture on a
large platter. Slice each tomato and each egg into four slices.
Arrange fried patties on lettuce, top each with a slice of tomato
and a slice of hard-boiled egg. Decorate with parsley sprigs.
Serve. Time: 50 min. Serves 4.

COCONUT SWEET

1 7-oz. can coconut
2 c. milk
1-3/4 c. sugar
1 stick cinnamon

3 egg yolks
2 T. butter
1/4 c. sliced unblanched
   almonds

Method: Place one cup of the milk, the sugar and the cinnamon
over moderate heat in a large pan; when it begins to boil, add the
coconut and stir until coconut looks transparent. Add the yolks
beaten with the rest of the milk, and stir constantly "until you
can see the bottom of the pan"—that is, until a wide swath of
pan appears every time you move the spoon through the mixture. Butter a large platter. Empty the mixture on it, sprinkle
with the almonds, and cool. Serve hot or cold, as you wish.
Time: 20 min. Serves 10-16 *small* portions. This is *very* rich—
and very good.

Menu 10

Zucchini Soup
Bananas in Wine
Frijoles
Chongos

Pork with Orange Sauce
Asparagus in Almond Sauce
Tortillas or French Bread
Coffee

ZUCCHINI SOUP

6 large tender zucchini
1 quart whole milk
4 T. butter

1 t. salt
1/2 to 3/4 t. black pepper
Oyster crackers (optional)

Method: Wash whole zucchini and parboil unpeeled in water to
barely cover, until fork-tender, about ten minutes. Remove
zucchini and discard stems. Crush zucchini roughly with fork or
potato masher. Leave some lumps. Return to cooking water,
with milk, butter, salt and pepper. Bring to boiling point. Serve.
Similar to oyster soup, this takes equally well to oyster crackers
or crisp soda crackers. Time: 20 min. Serves 6.

LOIN OF PORK WITH ORANGE SAUCE

1 large pork roast 5-6 lbs.
1/2 lb. raw ham, cubed
6 sweet oranges, juiced, or
   1 can frozen concentrate
1 t. salt
1 t. pepper
1 T. Worcestershire sauce

1 c. dry red wine, *or* cider
   vinegar, *or* cider
1 c. blanched almonds
1/2 c. raisins
1 t. instant coffee
Boiling water as needed

Method: Lard the loin with the ham cubes. Press them in as
firmly as possible. (About 20 min.) Place roast in deep roasting
pan and cover with the juice (reconstituted if not fresh), salt and
pepper. Let stand at least an hour; turn over once. Add wine and
Worcestershire sauce. Cover and bake at 350° until very tender,
allowing 25 to 30 minutes per pound. Thirty minutes before
serving, place the almonds and raisins in blender with some
of the pan juices and thoroughly grind them, adding the coffee.

Pour over the roast and stir into pan juices. If too thick, thin with a little boiling water. Cover and continue cooking. Thirty minutes later the sauce should have the consistency of a thick gravy. If too thin, grind a slice of bread and add to thicken, stir well and cook about 5 min. more. Serves 12-15.

BANANAS IN WINE

6 red cooking bananas, or underripe bananas, peeled, cut in half, and halved lengthwise

1/4 c. butter (1/2 stick)
1/2 c. sugar
1 c. red wine

Method: In a large pan heat butter over medium heat. Fry banana slices on each side until they brown. Time depends on size and variety of bananas, state of ripeness, and heat applied. Probably 15 minutes. Place slices fried first in deep bowl to conserve heat, and when all are fried, add the sugar to the pan and stir briskly until all the sugar melts (be careful not to burn). When sugar has caramelized, add the wine (if you warm it first it will sputter less.) Turn heat low and return all bananas to the pan to simmer until the sugar melts into the wine; 15 min. or less —then remove bananas again to deep, warm serving dish and pour the syrup over them. Serve at once. This is a vegetable here, but makes a good dessert, too. Time: 30 min. Serves 6.

ASPARAGUS WITH ALMOND SAUCE

1 bunch new asparagus, *or* 1 large can asparagus tips, or 1 pkg. frozen asparagus
1/8 c. cooking oil or butter
10 unpeeled almonds
4 little green onions, minced
1 large onion, minced

2 slices dark whole wheat bread (best, but white serves)
2 sprigs parsley
1/2 c. water
1 t. salt

Method: Wash asparagus and snap off woody ends of stalks. Cook until tender. A large coffee pot is ideal for cooking asparagus—put in enough water to boil the hard ends, and let rest of stalks steam. (15 min.) *Sauce:* Heat shortening and fry almonds to a dark brown. Remove almonds and in same fat fry the bread until golden on both sides. You may have to add more shortening. Remove bread and set pan aside. Grind bread and almonds together, with 1/2 c. water. Return pan to heat, replenish oil or butter if needed, and gently sauté the finely minced onions (include some of small onions' green stalks) until transparent (3-5 min.) Add the bread and almond mixture, minced parsley, and salt. Bring to a quick boil, reduce heat and simmer 10 minutes, or until thick. Serve very hot over well-drained asparagus. Time: 40 min. Serves 6.

FRIJOLES WITH TORTILLAS OR FRENCH BREAD

Recipes in Menu 3 for Frijoles Refritos and Tortillas. Should you prefer bread, use French bread from any good bakery or market. Whichever you use, have everything piping hot.

CHONGOS

This is an old-fashioned Mexican dessert, that used to be much in favor, especially on ranches where milk was plentiful. If too simple for your taste, a few tablespoonsful of your favorite liqueur—creme de cacao, anisette—will lend it sophistication. Stir into Chongos syrup just before serving.

1 quart milk	3/4 to 1 c. sugar
2 egg yolks	1 inch stick cinnamon,
2 junket tablets (rennet)	splintered

Method: In a 2 qt. pot heat the milk quickly to lukewarm; while it warms, beat the yolks in mixer or blender. Stir them into the milk, and add the rennet dissolved in 1 T. of water. (Junket tablets are hard to find unflavored; if your supermarket doesn't yield them, try the drug store.) Stir hard briefly, and pour into deep pan or pot about 8" x 8" or 10", and 3" or more deep, or pot about 8"-10" in diameter. Let set without moving until firm. Slice into squares with knife (16 squares). Sprinkle sugar and cinnamon over it and place over low heat to barely simmer 2 hours, or until curds have slightly-cheese-like consistency, (taste a small bit) and syrup thickens. Serve in attractive dish. Not counting time in firming: about 7 minutes. Serves 8.

Menu 11

White Bean Soup

Eggplant Acapulco   Tidbits for the Cardinal

Coffee

WHITE BEAN SOUP

2 c. white beans	1-1/2 t. salt
3 strips of bacon	1/4 t. pepper
2 c. tomato pulp	2 slices bread
1 brown onion, minced	2 T. butter

Method: Soak beans overnight. Cook in same water three hours, or until tender. If more water is needed to keep beans covered, be sure it is boiling. Drain beans; return liquid to pot. Blenderize beans a cupful at a time, adding some of their liquid to make blending easy. Return to pot. Fry bacon until crisp, and drain. Reserve the fat. Buzz the tomato and onion in the blender. Heat two tablespoonsful of the bacon fat and simmer the tomato mixture until it thickens, about ten minutes. Add to soup. Cut the bread into small cubes, heat the butter, and fry the bread, stirring, until golden—3 to 5 min. Add with crumbled bacon to soup and serve at once. Grated white cheese—Romano or Parmesan—is excellent with this soup, and if your family likes onions, small green ones, whole or minced, are a splendid addition. Time, exclusive of soaking beans: 3 hrs. 25 min. Serves 8.

LIVER AND RICE

4 T. cooking oil	1 bay leaf
1/2 lb. liver	1 pinch of orégano
1/2 lb. rice	1 t. salt
1 clove garlic	1 brown onion, minced
1 dry red chile pepper	3 c. hot broth or water
or 1 T. chile powder	

Method: Heat the oil and brown the liver, garlic, chile, bay leaf, orégano, salt and onion. Add the rice. Add the hot water or broth. Remove to a well-buttered casserole and bake in a 350° oven an hour, or more if you want it thicker. Time: 1 hour, 10 min. Serves 4.

EGGPLANT ACAPULCO

1 large eggplant	3 T. butter
1 large brown onion, minced	1 c. bread crumbs
1 clove garlic, minced	6 T. grated Romano cheese
2 sprigs parsley, minced	1/8 t. pepper, 1/2 t. salt

Method: Slice eggplant in half lengthwise. Soak halves one hour in salted water. Remove and plunge into boiling water, cover, and parboil ten minutes. Remove, drain, cool. Peel and mince the onion, garlic and parsley (omit stems). Heat butter and sauté the onion, garlic and parsley until onion is transparent (7 min.). Measure 3/4 of the crumbs into a bowl, and mix in the onion mixture. Carefully remove eggplant pulp to leave shells about 1/2 inch thick. Chop pulp and combine with the crumbs, 3 T. of the cheese, salt and pepper. Butter a casserole and arrange the shells in it. Fill shells with eggplant mixture, mounding well; combine remaining cheese and crumbs and pat over the tops of the mounds. Bake in 350° oven until crumbs are nicely browned (20 min.). Time exclusive of soaking: 45 min. Serves 2 generously, 4 amply—and can stretch to 6.

TIDBITS FOR THE CARDINAL

Cake:	Syrup:
4 eggs, separated	2 c. sugar
1/2 c. sugar	1 c. water
1/4 c. corn starch	
1/4 c. cake flour	
1 c. sherry	

Method: Preheat oven to 350°. In large bowl beat 4 egg whites very stiff. In small bowl, beat yolks until lemony, add sugar and continue beating. When stiff, add slowly, by tablespoonsful, the corn starch and cake flour. Carefully fold yolk mixture into beaten whites. Place in well-buttered pan (8" x 8" x2"). Bake 15 min. Turn off oven, slightly open door, and allow cake to cool in oven to prevent falling. When cold, cut into 16 squares. Arrange in a pretty bowl and slowly saturate with sherry. This requires about 1 cupful. Make syrup by bringing water and sugar to boil, and cook 5 minutes. Cook before pouring over cake. Refrigeration makes it even better. Time: 35 min. Serves 8.

Menu 12

FORMAL CHRISTMAS MENU

Oxtail Soup   Roast Goose or Turkey, Apple Dressing
Potatoes Paradise   Peas with Lettuce
      Frijoles   Zara's Ice Cream

OXTAIL SOUP

The beauty of this soup for a holiday menu is that it may be made the day before and reheated . . . and it is delicious.

1 oxtail	1 medium onion, finely
2 qts. water	minced
2 c. cooked and ground	1/4 t. pepper
garbanzo, *or* 1 15-oz. can,	1/2 to 1 T. finely minced
drained	parsley
1/4 c. cooking oil	Lemon wedges and/or chile
1 t. salt	sauce

Method: Place oxtail in water to boil. When it comes to a boil, reduce heat, and cook until meat is tender—at least two hours. Cool. Pick meat from bones and discard bones and excess fat. Return meat to broth. If you cook the garbanzos yourself, soak them overnight. Change waters and boil until tender and easily crushed between fingers. Drain. Buzz in blender with a little of the broth. Add garbanzos to meat. Heat cooking oil and fry onion until golden brown, and add. There should be about eight cups of soup; if necessary, add a little hot water. Season with salt and pepper. Bring to boiling point, add parsley, and serve, passing lemon wedges and chile sauce to enhance flavors. Time: With canned garbanzo, 2-1/2 hours. Serves 8-10.

ROAST GOOSE OR TURKEY

Goose is used only occasionally in Mexico; turkey is *the* holiday bird. If you doubt your ability to select a good bird, ask the butcher to help you. Fowl freshly killed is the best, but if you buy yours frozen, allow plenty of time for defrosting or you'll have meat done on the outside with dressing and meat near bones uncooked. To prepare fowl, wipe it carefully inside and out with clean damp cloth. Rub with salt. Examine for overlooked pin feathers and singe them off with a lighted match or candle; pluck dark ends of other overlooked feathers with tweezers. Allow 1 lb. of uncooked turkey for each 2 people.

APPLE DRESSING

1/2 lb. prunes, pitted
1/2 lb. blanched almonds, halved
10 green apples (pippins) peeled, cored, and slightly cooked in
1/4 lb. butter (1 stick)

1/2 lb. pound cake, crumbled
1 t. sugar
1 t. salt
1/4 t. pepper
1/2 t. nutmeg, fresh grated
2 c. cooking sherry (or apple cider)

Method: Boil prunes till soft and discard pits. Or buy pitted prunes and soak in water to barely cover until plump. Blanche shelled almonds by pouring boiling water on them; let stand five minutes, then pop them out of their skins. Slice in halves lengthwise. Prepare apples and cut in bite sizes. Warm butter over low heat in a large pan, and sauté apples until transparent and tinged with gold. Add cake crumbles (not crumbs!), almonds, prunes, sugar, salt, pepper, nutmeg, and sherry. Mix and stir. Cool. (1 hour.) Stuff fowl with this mixture, sew up openings, and roast without peaking. Bake 3-1/2 to 4 hours for a turkey 6-8 lbs. 7 to 8-1/4 for one 20-24 lbs., (before stuffing). Add about 1-1/4 hours for each extra four lbs. When well done, leg should be easy to move back and forth. Young goose, 30 min. per lb. 300° oven.

POTATOES PARADISE

6 medium potatoes, boiled,
    peeled, mashed
1/2 c. butter (1 stick)
1/2 c. sugar
1/2 c. grated white dry cheese
    (Parmesan, Romano)

1 c. milk
4 eggs, beaten
1 t. salt
1/2 t. pepper
1/2 c. bread crumbs

Method: Slowly and in the following order stir into the mashed potatoes the butter, sugar, cheese, milk, beaten yolks, salt and pepper, then fold in stiffly beaten whites. Liberally butter a casserole and pat all the bread crumbs into the butter. Pour in the potato mix and place in the oven at 350° in a large pan of hot water. Bake 1 to 1-1/2 hours until golden on top and firmly set (test it as you might a cake). Run a spatula around edge of potatoes, and unmold carefully onto a large platter. Delicious! Time: 1 hr. 45 min. to 2 hrs. 15 min. Serves 8-10.

PEAS WITH LETTUCE

This is even better if you have a herb garden and can use a sprig of fresh basil; but if you haven't, you'll find dried basil at any good market.

1/8 lb. butter (1/2 stick)
1/2 head iceberg lettuce,
    chopped
1 pkg. frozen peas
1/2 t. sugar

1/4 t. pepper
1/2 t. sweet basil
1/2 c. beef or chicken broth
    or consommé
1/4 c. red wine (dry)

Method: Melt butter in bottom of casserole with cover in which you will cook and serve this. Add lettuce, peas, sugar, pepper, basil, and broth. Cover and simmer over low heat until broth is absorbed, about 20 minutes. Add wine, cover and cook 3 minutes more, and serve. Very good. Time: 25 minutes. Serves 6.

FRIJOLES
(Recipe in Menu 3)

ZARA'S ICE CREAM

1 can evaporated milk
2 egg whites, beaten

1 small jar maraschino
   cherries (4 oz.)

Method: Blend milk (chilled in refrigerator) and cherries and their liquid in blender, only for a moment or two: cherries should not be too well blended. Thoroughly whip egg whites, fold in cherry mixture. Freeze to desired consistency. If you like a stronger flavor, add from 1/2 to 1 t. almond extract. Time: 2-1/2 hours. Serves 6.

Menu 13

INFORMAL HOLIDAY MENU

Spareribs in Green Chile   Lazy Enchiladas
Christmas Salad   Marquesote
Rompope   Coffee
Anisette

SPARERIBS IN GREEN CHILE

Method: To each 3 or 4 lbs. of spareribs allow one bottle of La
Victoria green taco sauce. (If you prefer the red, use it.) Allow
about 1/2 lb. per person if using this recipe as the main course. If
following this complete menu, two ribs per person will do. Buy
them farmer style, with plenty of meat. Ask the butcher to chop
them into two inch lengths, or do it yourself with a cleaver and
sharp knife. Wash to remove any bone splinters. Dry. Heat oven
to 350°. Place ribs in a large covered baking pan. If ribs are lean,
add a little cooking oil at bottom of the pan. Bake for an hour,
or until brown. Uncover and cook ten minutes more. Remove
pan from oven and cover ribs with chile sauce. Return to oven for
10 minutes more—15 if sauce is very cold—until sauce bubbles.
The meat should be very tender, the fat practically turned to
"cracklin's," and the sauce thick. Serve with hot tortillas. Time:
1 hr. 15 min.

LAZY ENCHILADAS

1 can tomato soup	1/2 c. finely sliced green
3 eggs	onions
1 t. salt	Cooking oil
2 T. chile powder	1 dozen fresh tortillas
1/2 c. grated Romano cheese	Lettuce finely sliced

Method: In blender or mixer, combine tomato soup, eggs, salt
and chile powder. Prepare cheese and onions and mix together
in small bowl. In large pan over medium heat, heat the oil. Start
with 3 tablespoonsful and add as needed. It requires about 1 T.
per tortilla. Dip tortillas quickly into the soup and egg sauce, and
fry 1-1/2 min. on each side—only until egg is cooked. Remove
tortilla to platter with lettuce on it, sprinkle down the middle

with onion-cheese, roll up and resprinkle with same mixture. If desired these may be made ahead and kept hot in warm oven for 15 to 20 min., then transferred to their lettuce bed. Time: 30 min. Serves 6.

ADELITA'S CHRISTMAS SALAD
YOLK SALAD DRESSING

8 hard-boiled yolks	1/8 t. pepper
3 T. olive oil	1/4 c. vinegar
6 T. claret	1 t. salt
2 T. dry mustard	1 t. sugar
1 finely chopped green onion	

Method: Hard boil eggs, 6 min. at least. Mash yolks. Combine with the olive oil, claret, mustard, onion, and pepper. Let stand half an hour. Strain. Add vinegar, salt and sugar. Taste to correct seasoning. Refrigerate until needed. (10 minutes).

CHRISTMAS SALAD

For each person:	Round avocado slice
Lettuce leaves	Pomegranate seeds (optional)
Large tomato slice	Yolk Salad Dressing
Guacamole (p. 125)	Radish rose
or	
Minced onion	

Method: On a large saucer or bread and butter plate, arrange one or more lettuce leaves. Place large tomato slice in center. Place avocado slice on tomato. Fill center of avocado slice with guacamole *or* minced onion. Pour Yolk Salad Dressing over the mound, and sprinkle with pomegranate seeds. Adorn with a radish rose at side. Time: about 15 minutes for 6 people.

MARQUESOTE

This extremely fine and elegant cake used to be traditional in Mexico, at weddings and other very special occasions.

6 egg whites	1 c. powdered sugar
2 c. whipping or all purpose cream	1/2 c. cake flour
	1 t. vanilla

44

Method: Heavily butter a square pan (8" x 8" x 2"). Heat oven to 250°. Beat whites until very stiff. Beat cream stiff, and add sugar to it a little at a time, folding it in until all the sugar is used. Now fold the whites into the cream mixture by the large spoonful, very carefully, alternating with spoonsful of the 3-times-sifted flour, and the vanilla. Work as lightly and gently as you can. Pour into the buttered pan and bake about 1-1/2 hours, until pail golden on top. *Don't* peek: it falls easily. At the end of the time, open the oven door cautiously and look; if golden, test with thin sharp knife; if it comes out clean, cake is done. If in doubt, give it more time. When satisfied that it is done, close door very gently and let it cool where it is. Cold, cut it into lady finger strips to serve. The bottom is jellylike; the top like meringue. Time: 2 hours. Makes 16 fingers.

ROMPOPE

This delicious Mexican holiday drink is a cross between American eggnog and Tom and Jerry . . . and yet is very different!

1 pint milk (evaporated)	2 egg yolks
1 c. sugar	1 c. brandy
2 T. ground blanched almonds	2 drops nutmeg essence or essence of cloves (buy at drug store)
3 inches stick cinnamon, crushed	

Method: Bring milk with the sugar, almonds, and cinnamon to a boil. Boil five minutes, stirring to dissolve sugar. Cool twenty minutes; beat in the egg yolks. Strain. Add the brandy and essence of nutmeg or cloves. Pour into a bottle and refrigerate. Serve in small cups or liqueur glasses. Time: about 15 min.

ANISETTE

This you may buy at any liquor store—but it's fun to make.

Method: Boil together four cups of sugar and four cups of water until syrupy (25-30 min.) Cool. Have ready two wine bottles (fifths). Pour half the syrup in each. When wholly cold, finish filling with vodka. Add 60 drops of essence of anise (buy at drug store), or a teaspoonful of anise flavoring. Time: 2 hours 10 min.

Pomegranate Chicken   Drowned Cauliflower
Green Corn Casserole   Tipsy Apples
Coffee

POMEGRANATE CHICKEN

1 large tender stewing hen   1/4 t. cinnamon
1/4 c. cooking oil   Pinch of saffron
1 medium can tomatoes,   1/4 c. blanched almonds
    sieved   1/4 c. raisins
1 c. chicken broth   1 c. Malaga wine
1/4 t. ground cloves   Seeds of 1 pomegranate
1/4 t. pepper   Avocado (optional)

Method: Disjoint chicken. Heat oil and lightly fry chicken until brown on all sides. (30 minutes.) Add tomatoes, broth, spices, almonds and raisins. Cover, reduce heat. Boil gently till meat is tender and sauce thickened (25 minutes). Add wine, simmer 5 minutes more. If sauce is soupy, quickly grind 1 or 2 slices of white bread in blender and add to thicken. Remove to platter, pour sauce around it, and sprinkle with pomegranate seeds. Garnish with avocado slices. 1 hour. Serves 6.

DROWNED CAULIFLOWER

2 large onions   1 avocado, peeled, seeded, in
1 large cauliflower   strips
2 cloves garlic   1/2 t. orégano
1 t. salt   2 T. olive oil
2 T. cooking oil   4 to 6 chiles serranos (buy
1/2 c. seeded green olives   canned; *very hot* peppers!)

Method: Boil big onions about 20 minutes, until tender. Cut in half through stem end and separate into "petals." At the same time but not in same pot parboil cauliflower. When tender, drain it and carefully separate into florets. Cut the large florets in half through stem and blossom, as the more seasoning they absorb, the better they taste. Dry with paper towels. Mince garlic and rub with the salt to a paste in a mortar. In large pan heat cooking oil and sauté the garlic paste until golden. Push to one side. Add florets to heated oil, and sauté over medium heat until golden. Turn often to prevent burning. Remove to a casserole or pretty bowl, arranging them stem downward. Drizzle remaining garlic and oil over them. Sprinkle with onion petals, olives, and avocado slices. Rubbing orégano between your palms, sprinkle it on the florets. Drizzle with olive oil. Arrange chiles serranos around bowl. This is delicious—even garlic-haters ask for more. And it is very good left-over, should any survive. Time: 45 minutes. Serves 8.

GREEN CORN CASSEROLE

3 ears of tender young green
   corn or 1 can cream style
   corn (large)
1 c. milk, evaporated
   preferred

1 t. sugar
1 t. salt
1 inch stick cinnamon
3 eggs, separated

Method: Slice tender young corn from ears, or use a large can of cream style corn. Cook in milk to barely cover, with sugar, salt and cinnamon, 15 minutes over low heat. Stir to prevent sticking. Beat egg whites until stiff, add yolks one at a time, still beating. Discard cinnamon stick. Gently fold corn mixture into the eggs. Pour into a well-buttered 6 cup casserole. Set in pan of hot water and bake at 350° until golden brown and firm . . . 1 hour. Serve in casserole. Time: 1 hour, 20 min. Serves 8.

TIPSY APPLES

6 good cooking apples
2 c. sugar
Juice of 1/2 lemon

1/2 stick cinnamon, slivered
2 c. dry red wine

Method: Peel and core apples, placing in cold water with lemon juice to prevent discoloring. Remove to ovenproof casserole with lid. (You can make one of aluminum foil.) Fill apple cavities with sugar and pour remaining sugar over them. Sprinkle with slivered cinnamon. Pour wine around apples. Cover and bake at 250°, 2 hours at least. Serve warm (not hot), or chilled, with cream or without. Serves 6.

Menu 15

Roast Duck a la María   Apple Sauce
Claret   Stuffed Chayote
Orange Cup   Coffee

ROAST DUCK A LA MARIA

When I lived in Mexico, our ducks were wild, and we usually allowed one duck for each two people. Should you buy domesticated ducks, allow for the large amount of fat they carry.

Preliminary step, for wild ducks only: Stuff a large onion into the body cavity of each duck, and parboil in boiling water for 1/2 hour. Remove from liquid, drain, cool, discard onions and dry the ducks.

STUFFING *(for one duck)*

2 parboiled medium potatoes, peeled and diced finely
2 carrots, parboiled, diced small
2 turnips, parboiled, diced small

2 raw zucchini, diced small
1 medium onion, chopped fine and fried in 2 T. butter
1 or 2 small red peppers
Bacon strips

Method: Parboil potatoes, carrots, and turnips; peel and dice very small-about 1/2 inch. Peel and chop onion fine and fry in hot butter until transparent. Remove and discard stems on peppers. Break peppers into small bits. If you object to hot seasonings, let them stay whole, but warn eaters to watch for them and discard them. But do include them; they impart a special flavor to the stuffing. Add onion, peppers, and thin sliced zucchini to the other vegetables. Wash and chop fine the giblets and add to stuffing, and mix with 1 teaspoonful of salt. If domesticated duck, wash inside and out and dry with paper towels; salt and pepper all over, inside and out. Stuff the body cavity with the vegetable mix, and sew. Then stuff as much as possible into the neck skin cavity and either sew it up or fold the large flap of neck skin over the opening and tie it down with a stout cord around the duck's body. Very lightly grease roaster and place duck in it. Arrange strips of bacon lengthwise over breast-side of body, and secure with toothpicks at each end, to discard before serving. Use two smaller strips to fasten across the long ones. Cover and roast in preheated 300° oven 2 hours. You will find the duck is done, the pan has a great deal of grease in it, and if you wish you can serve the duck now. But replace the lid, reduce heat to 150°, and cook 1/2 hour more. Then remove roaster lid and bake yet another 1/2 hour . . . a total of three hours. This produces a truly succulent, grease-free, tender duck. Time: 3 hrs. 45 min. Serves 4.

STUFFED CHAYOTES

4 or 5 chayotes (large)
1/2 lb. cooked kid or lamb,
   shredded (pork and ham
   also good)
1 small onion, minced

4 T. butter
2 eggs
1 c. crumbs
1 t. salt
1/2 t. pepper

Method: Allow one chayote for each two people. Drop chayotes into boiling water and boil till fork-tender, 15-20 minutes. Drain and cool. Slice lengthwise into halves. With spoon scoop out pulp and seeds, leaving shell about 1/2 inch thick. Be careful not to break it. Chop the pulp and seeds with the shredded meat. Mince the onion, heat the butter, and fry the onion until golden (6 min.). Add to the chayote mixture with the two eggs, whites and yolks separately beaten to stiffness, half the crumbs, salt and pepper. Mix well and fill the shells, mounding the mixture. Pat remaining crumbs over tops. Bake in 350° oven until nicely browned, 20-25 min. Serves 8-10. If chayotes are not in season, large zucchini may be successfully used.

ORANGE CUP

This simple, easy-to-make mixture is a delightful *aperitif* before meals, or may be used as a *finale*, as here. Allow one fine orange per person. Peel and segment fruit, remove all membranes; break each segment into bite-sizes. For each orange allow 3 to 4 fresh mint leaves, minced fine. Allow 2 T. honey to each. Combine honey and mint leaves and pour over the oranges, stir well, and chill. Serve in attractive glass bowls or stem ware. Time: 10-15 min. for 6. Serves 6 generously, 8 adequately.

Menu 16

Carrot Soup   Lentils with Escabeche
Colache   Lemon Banana Cloud
Coffee

CARROT SOUP

1 large onion, minced
1/2 medium can tomatoes or
  2 tomatoes, diced

4 to 6 large carrots
4 to 6 c. water or consommé
1/4 c. cooking oil

Method: Mince onion, dice tomatoes. Wash carrots and remove any imperfections. Place water or consommé to boil. Sauté onion in heated oil until tender and transparent; add tomatoes and simmer until thick. Add tomato mixture and carrots (whole, unpeeled) to broth, or boiling water. When carrots are fork-tender, remove and crush them roughly with a fork and return to soup. Salt and pepper to taste. Time: 30 min. Serves 8.

LENTILS IN ESCABECHE

4 large onions, peeled, sliced,
  with rings separated
1 c. vinegar
1/4 c. olive oil
1 t. salt
1 clove garlic

1/4 t. pepper
2-6 tiny red peppers
1 lb. largest lentils
Water to cover
Salt
2 T. olive oil

Method: Prepare onions in escabeche the day before. Slice onions and separate into rings, then put to soak in the vinegar, olive oil, salt, garlic, pepper and peppers. If you do not care for hot peppers, leave them whole; if you enjoy chiles, break them into tiny bits. The following day boil the lentils 1-2 hours, or until tender. Boil gently to keep them whole. Do not salt until they are thoroughly done. Add salt to taste. Drain, and reserve liquid for soup. Place drained lentils on a large platter, with some depth. Drain the onions and spread them over the lentils. Sprinkle with 2 T. olive oil. Time: 2 hours. Serves 10-12, delicious hot or cold.

COLACHE

1 t. butter or cooking oil
1 large onion, finely minced
1 c. string beans, in inch
   lenghts, or 1/2 pkg. frozen
   string beans
2 large peeled tomatoes,
   cubed, or 1 to 1-1/2 c. canned
   tomatoes, crushed

5 zucchini, sliced in rounds
1 chile verde, chopped
4 ears corn, cut from ears, or
   2 cans whole kernel, or 1
   can cream style
1 t. salt
1/4 t. pepper

Method: Heat the butter and cook the onion until golden. Add string beans, zucchini, chile, tomatoes and corn, cover and simmer until vegetables are tender, about 1/2 hour. Add salt and pepper. Taste to correct seasoning. Use low heat and stir several times, but do not cook dry. Time: 35 min. Serves 8.

LEMON BANANA CLOUD

4 egg whites
1/2 c. sugar
3 very ripe mashed bananas

Grated rind of 1 lemon
1 t. vanilla

Method: Beat egg whites until very stiff. Still beating, add sugar in slow dribbles, banana pulp, also slowly, grated rind and vanilla. Pour gently into buttered casserole and bake at 350° until set and brown on top—20-30 min. Serve cold. Better if made the day before serving. Time: 30 minutes. Serves 6.

Menu 17

Caldo Acapulco
Chiles in Nut Sauce

Chicken with Orange Sauce
Niño Envuelto

Coffee

CALDO ACAPULCO

Soup:
2 T. cooking oil
1 medium onion, finely minced
2 c. Tomatoes, diced

Noodles:
1/2 c. Masa Harina
1 t. chile powder
1/2 t. salt

6 sprigs cilantro (Chinese parsley; coriander herb) *or* pinch of orégano
4 c. boiling water or consommé

1/8 c. cooking fat
1/2 c. water

Method: Heat the oil and gently sauté the onion until golden. Add tomatoes and simmer until thick, 10 minutes. Buzz the mixture in your blender or press through sieve. Add cilantro, stems discarded, finely minced. Bring consommé to a boil, add tomato mixture. Let it simmer while you make the noodles: Sift the Masa Harina, chile powder, salt and baking powder, or simply stir them in a bowl with a spoon. Add water a little at a time and stir thoroughly; you want a stiff dough. Pat dough into thin tortillas, about 3 inches across. Spread on bread board to dry for 1/2 hour. Slice into strips 1/2 inch wide. Heat remaining cooking fat; fry strips golden brown. Keep hot and add to soup at the moment of serving. Time: 45 min. Serves 6.

CHICKEN IN ORANGE SAUCE

Chicken, about 3 lbs., disjointed
Salt, pepper
3 T. butter
1/2 c. blanched almonds
1/2 c. seedless raisins
1/4 t. nutmeg
1 t. salt

1/4 t. pepper
1/4 t. cinnamon
1/4 t. cloves
1 small can pineapple chunks, drained, or fresh chunks
2 c. fresh or frozen reconstituted orange juice
2 T. flour

52

Method: Sprinkle the chicken with salt and pepper. Brown the chicken in the heated butter (medium flame) add the almonds, raisins, nutmeg, salt, pepper, cinnamon and cloves, pineapple and orange juice. Cover and simmer about 40 minutes. Mix the flour with a very little cold water until smooth, and put through a sieve into the pan juices. Cook and stir until thick, about 5 minutes longer. Time: 1 hour, 20 min. Serves 4-6.

CHILES IN NUT SAUCE

For this recipe, try to obtain long green mildly hot chiles poblanos; or use 2 4-oz. cans of Ortega's whole Green Chiles. If you use fresh chiles, roast them ten minutes in a hot oven. Remove and wrap in a towel to steam 10 minutes. Unwrap, slit lengthwise, remove all seeds and interior white membrane. Try not to break the peppers. Place them, whether canned or steamed, in a bowl and cover with vinegar to steep at least six hours. Drain, stuff with Picadillo Filling and top with Nut Sauce. 2 cans of chiles verdes serve 6 people.

PICADILLO

1/4 lb. ground beef	2 zucchini, finely diced
1/4 lb. ground pork, *unseasoned*	1 carrot, finely diced
	1 medium potato, finely diced
2 T. cooking oil	A pinch of orégano
1/2 c. finely minced onion	Salt and pepper to taste
1 c. tomato, chopped	

Method: Mix together the beef and pork, and cook in the heated cooking oil with the onion, stirring and breaking up meat while it cooks so that it is well frizzled. Add the tomato, zucchini, carrot, potato, orégano (rubbed between your palms), and salt and pepper to taste. Cover and simmer until thick, 20 to 30 minutes. Cool. Stuff into peppers, to serve at once; or to cool, refrigerate, and serve later.

NUT SAUCE

1/2 c. unblanched almonds	1 t. sugar
1/2 c. walnut or pecan meats	1/8 c. salad oil
1/4 c. water	1/8 c. vinegar
1/4 t. salt	

Method: Blenderize nut meats with the water, salt and sugar. Add the oil and vinegar and buzz half a minute more. Spoon over the peppers. Time for Chiles with Nut Sauce: 1 hour 15 min. Serves 6-8.

NIÑO ENVUELTO

1/2 c. melted butter, cooled	3/4 c. flour
5 eggs	Prune or peach jam
1/2 c. sugar	

Method: Melt and cool butter. Beat yolks and whites separately until stiff. Combine and still beating, slowly add sugar, sifted flour, and melted butter. On baking sheet place waxed paper. Butter paper. Spread dough about 1/2 inch thick over the paper. Bake at 350° about 50 min.-1 hour. When cake tester comes out clean, remove cake from oven and roll up quickly, paper and all. Wrap in a towel. Let rest 15-20 min. Unwrap, carefully loosening paper, but leaving it under the cake. Spread the cake with jam, reroll, discarding waxed paper. Roll entire cake in powdered sugar. Cut off both ends for neat appearance. Slice about one inch thick to serve. This Mexican jelly roll—"Bundled-up Baby"—is particularly good with coffee. Serves 12-15.

PRUNE JAM

1 lb. prunes, pitted preferred	1 inch stick of cinnamon
1-1/2 c. water	1 lemon peeled, slightly rubbed
1-1/2 c. sugar	with grater

Method. Bring all ingredients quickly to a boil, and cook ten minutes. Remove, and discard peel, cinnamon, and prune pits. Blenderize prunes, adding syrup a tablespoonful or two at a time, only until mixture becomes a thick paste. Time: 12 min.

Menu 18

Frijol Soup
Green Chicken

Sopa de Jocoque
Artichokes in Escabeche

Pineapple Sherbert

FRIJOL SOUP

4 to 6 c. pinto or pink bean
broth
1 to 2 c. puréed beans
2 T. cooking oil or bacon fat
1 large onion, minced
2 c. tomatoes, peeled and
puréed or chopped
1/2 t. orégano *or* 2 or 3 sprigs
of parsley minced fine, *or*
both

Croutons, 2 T. for each
serving, *or* large slice of
French bread fried, for
each serving, 2 T. butter
for each slice
Grated Romano and/or
Parmesan cheese

Method: Follow recipe for cooking frijoles (Menu 3). Drain and measure 6 c. broth to return to pot. If you don't have enough, add hot water to extend broth. Purée beans in blender and add to pot. Heat cooking oil or fat, sauté the onion until transparent, add tomatoes and simmer ten minutes, until thick. Add orégano, rubbed between your palms, or parsley. Now add tomato mixture to soup. Bring to boil, reduce heat, and continue boiling gently about 5 minutes. Serve. Place croutons of fried bread in serving bowl, or individual soup bowls, and pour soup over them. Either add the cheese at once, or pass it, as you prefer. Time, exclusive of bean cooking time: 20 min. Serves 10.

SOPA DE JOCOQUE

2 c. cooking oil or bacon
drippings
2 large onions, minced
1 or 2 cloves garlic, finely
minced
1 # 2-1/2 can tomatoes, crushed
2 dozen fresh corn tortillas

1 lb. Cheddar cheese, 1/8 in.
thick slices
4 oz. can Ortega green chiles,
sliced in strips
4 oz. can pimentos, sliced
1 qt. buttermilk
Salt, as desired (about 1 T.)

Method: Preheat oven to 350°. Grease liberally a large pan
(17" x 11-1/2" x 2-1/2"). Heat oil or drippings and sauté the
onions and garlic, add the tomatoes and cook until mixture
thickens, about 10 minutes. Place a layer of tortillas in the
bottom of the pan. You have to tear some of them in halves or
quarters to cover the bottom. Place a slice of cheese on each tortilla and parts of slices on torn sections; sprinkle all heavily with
sauce, lightly with salt; distribute a strip of chile and one of
pimento as you did the cheese; pour buttermilk over all to cover
thinly. Repeat the operation until all the tortillas are used, cover
with all of the leftover sauce, cover with all the buttermilk, and
arrange the prettiest slices of cheese, chiles and pimento in a
pleasing design on top. Place aluminum foil over the pan and
tuck in the edges to seal. Bake one hour. Remove foil during last
ten minutes to allow light browning. Time: 1 hour, 25 min.
Serves 6 heartily, unless used as a substitute for rice or potatoes at
a big meal: then it serves 12.

ARTICHOKES IN ESCABECHE

10 to 12 small artichokes	1/2 t. pepper
1/2 c. olive oil	1/2 t. orégano
1 c. vinegar	2 bay leaves
1 t. salt	2 cloves garlic
1 large onion, sliced thin	

Method: Prepare this several days before use. Select tiny artichokes, the completely edible kind. Hearts of older artichokes, or
canned hearts, may be used instead. Boil artichokes until just
tender. Drain. In olive oil, sauté the onion, salt, pepper, orégano
and bay leaves until onion is golden; add the artichokes and sauté
five minutes more. Then add the vinegar and garlic. Place all in
a covered utensil or jar. To serve, drain off the sauce, which may
then be used to flavor olives or for salads. Time: 20 minutes.
Serves 6-8.

GREEN CHICKEN

2 young fryers, disjointed
1/4 c. cooking oil
2 T. olive oil
1 t. salt
1 c. water
1 finely minced clove of
  garlic

4 T. finely minced onion
1 slice of white bread
6 sprigs parsley, finely
  minced
4 T. cooked peas
1 c. cooked peas

Method: Wash chicken and dry with paper towels. Heat cooking oil and fry chicken golden brown. Add water and salt, cover, reduce heat and simmer until tender, (abt. 45 min. for frying and simmering). In a second pan heat olive oil and fry onion and garlic until golden, about 5 min., push aside and fry bread on both sides. Blenderize the onion, garlic, bread, and 4 T. cooked peas, with a little water from the peas . . . about two tablespoonsful. Add with the whole peas to the chicken and simmer until thick, about 5 min. more. Serve. Time: 45 min. to 1 hour. Serves 8.

PINEAPPLE SHERBET

1 c. pineapple juice
1 can crushed pineapple
1/4 c. sugar

Juice of 1/2 lemon
4 egg whites, well beaten

Method: Combine pineapple juice, pineapple, sugar, and lemon juice. Stir to dissolve sugar. In freezer pans, freeze to a mush, 1 to 2 hours (you'll have to watch it). Remove and beat in your mixer. Return to refrigerator, beat the egg white very stiff, then combine the pineapple mush with the stiff egg whites and return to freezer again. 1-2 hours more. Preparation time, exclusive of freezing time: about 10 minutes. Serves 8.

Menu 19

Lentil Soup   Chicken a la Bella Mulata
Scrambled Carrots   Almendrado with Custard Cream

LENTIL SOUP

6-8 c. water
1 c. big lentils (1/2 lb.)
2 T. cooking oil
2 c. tomato pulp, canned or
    fresh

1 large onion, minced
3-5 tender zucchini
2 large, or 3 medium, *under-
    ripe* bananas
1-2 t. salt

Method: In large pot put cold water and lentils on high heat.
When boiling starts, reduce heat to medium. Cook two hours.
At end of 1-1/2 hours, heat cooking oil, fry onion until transparent, add tomato and cook 10-15 min. Empty into soup. If water
level has reduced greatly, add enough hot water to insure 6-8 c.
broth. Slice zucchini into soup. Remove both ends of bananas
and slice, *unpeeled,* in thin rounds into soup. Cover and continue gently boiling until serving time; add slat, taste, stir well
and serve. Make a guessing game: "What is in the soup?" Most
will guess artichokes! Time: 2 hours. Serves 8 twice, 16 once.

CHICKEN A LA BELLA MULATA

1 large stewing hen
Water to cover
1 t. salt
1/2 c. cooking oil
1/2 lb. pork backbone or spare
    ribs
1/4 c. unblanched almonds
2 thick slices French bread
2 cloves garlic ground with
    1 t. salt
1 medium onion, chopped

4 tomatoes, peeled and
    chopped
15 sprigs of parsley, minced
1 t. ground cinnamon
1/2 t. ground nutmeg
1/2 t. ground cloves
1/2 t. pepper
1 T. chile powder (mild
    or hot)
1 t. cumin seed, ground
1 t. coriander seed, ground
1 c. sherry

58

Method: In a four or five quart sauce pan, boil the disjointed hen with water to barely cover, and 1 t. salt, until well-done. In a very large pan, heat 1/2 c. cooking oil and fry the pork until nicely brown on all sides. Push to one side and fry the almonds until brown, then the bread. Blenderize almonds and bread. Add remaining oil to the pan. Crush garlic and salt together and fry with the onion until transparent; reduce heat and add tomatoes, parsley, cinnamon, nutmeg, cloves, pepper, chile powder, cumin and coriander seeds. Add almonds and bread, and a cup of chicken broth. Simmer until thick. Add the chicken to the sauce, and if necessary, another half cup or cup of broth. Simmer 25 minutes, or until thick, covered. Then add the sherry, cover, and simmer three minutes more, until it begins to bubble. Serve at once. Time: 1 hour. Serves 6-8.

SCRAMBLED CARROTS

4-5 carrots, boiled	1 medium tomato, minced
2 T. cooking oil	2-4 eggs
1 large onion, minced	1/2 t. salt

Method: Slice cooked carrots into thin disks. Heat oil. Brown onion in oil, add tomatoes and carrots, and cook gently until sauce begins to dry, about 10 minutes. Break eggs into bowl, add salt, stir quickly with fork and pour over the carrots. Stir and cook until dry, 5 to 10 minutes. Serve at once. Serves 6-8.

ALMENDRADO (From Mrs. Eleanor Gausewitz)

1 T. gelatine (1 env.)	1 c. almonds, blanched and
1/4 c. cold water	ground
5 egg whites	1/2 t. almond extract
1/2 c. sugar	Red and green food coloring

Method: Soften gelatine in cold water and set cup in hot water over low heat to dissolve. Beat whites stiff but not dry. Still beating, slowly dribble in the sugar, almond flavor, and gelatine, until the mixture peaks. Transfer 1/3 to another bowl. Gently sprinkle ground almonds over the remaining 2/3, and fold them in gently. Place half of this in a second small bowl. Carefully color the mixture in one bowl a delicate green, and that in the other red, using only enough tint to make the color definite. Line a loaf pan (8-1/2" x 4-1/2" x 3") with waxed paper, let some overlap ends of pan, to ease removing of dessert. Spoon the green layer into the pan, smooth it; spoon in the white layer and smooth; and follow with the red layer. Chill in refrigerator at least six hours. "Almonded" is the literal translation of *almendrado*. The colors are those of the Mexican flag. Slice gelatin in inch-thick portions to serve. Preparation time: 20 minutes. Serves 6. Top with custard cream.

CUSTARD CREAM

1 pint milk (2 c.)	Pinch of salt
5 egg yolks	1 T. vanilla
1/4 c. sugar	

Method: Mix milk, yolks, sugar and salt in the top of a double boiler over boiling water, and stir constantly. When mixture coats the spoon (about 15 min.) remove and cool about 15 min. more. Press through a sieve to remove hard bits of egg white. Beat in vanilla and cool. Chill in refrigerator. Beat the "crust" in before serving. Time: 15 min. Serves 6.

Menu 20

Chona's Albóndigas   Sherried Chicken Breasts
Cauliflower in Guacamole   Neapolitan Snow Pudding
Coffee

CHONA'S ALBONDIGAS

Caldo:
6-8 c. water
1 large soup bone
1/4 to 1/2 head cabbage, in
   wedges
1-2 large onions, quartered
1 tomato, cubed
10-15 sprigs cilantro (Chinese
   parsley) or parsley
2-3 cloves garlic
1/2 can garbanzo (optional)
Salt to taste

Albóndigas:
1 lb. chopped beef, *or*
1/2 lb. ground round and 1/2 lb.
   ground pork, unseasoned
6 sprigs fresh mint, stem
   discarded, finely minced *or*
   1/2 to 1 t. orégano, rubbed
   between palms

1/4 c. rice
1 egg
1 t. salt

Method: Make classic Mexican soup—caldo—in 5 to 8 qt. pot. In it put the water and soup bone, bring quickly to a boil, add all the other ingredients listed in first column, reduce heat and let boil gently until meat on bone is tender. For the albóndigas, combine the two meats (if you use pork also) in medium bowl, punch hole in center and into hole put the mint, rice and egg, then mix and squeeze by hand until ingredients are combined. Add salt and work again. Shape balls size of a large walnut. Drop into the boiling soup about 1/2 hour before serving time; cover pot. Serve albóndigas with hot French bread, hot tortillas, or both; also pass lemon wedges, chile sauce, and bananas to add to the soup if desired. If any remains for the next day, rejoice! Time: 1 hour. Serves 8.

SHERRIED CHICKEN BREASTS

8 chicken breasts
1/4 c. butter (1/2 stick)
1/2 c. sherry
4 medium onions, minced
1-2 cloves garlic, finely
 minced
4 T. parsley, minced
1 bay leaf
3 eggs well-beaten
1 c. bread crumbs

Sauce:
2 T. butter
2 T. finely sliced little green
 onions
2 T. flour
1 t. grated lemon peel
2 c. chicken consommé
1/4 c. sherry

Method: Over medium heat, fry the chicken breasts in butter until they are well-browned on all sides. Add sherry, onions, garlic, parsley and bay leaf and cover pan. Cook chicken until tender. (20 min.) Remove from heat and discard bay leaf. Remove chicken from sauce to cool until easy to handle, about 15 minutes. With a sharp knife, slit between breast and bone structure, creating a pocket which is stuffed with the drained mixture from pan. If necessary fasten with toothpicks to remove before serving. Beat egg whites stiff; still beating add one yolk at a time. Place crums in a shallow bowl. Dip chicken breasts first into egg and then into crumbs. Place on well-buttered cookie sheet, bone-side down, and slide them under 450° broiler for about 5 min., or until browned. Do not turn. Sauce: Melt 2 T. butter in medium sauce pan, add onions and flour, and stir together until onions are transparent and flour blended in. About 3 min. Add the consommé and cook till thick, stirring often— about 5 minutes. Add lemon peel and sherry, stir well, and let thicken again, about 3-5 min. more. Pour over chicken breasts and serve. Time: 50-55 min. Serves 4-8. (2 to a person, or 1 to a person.)

CAULIFLOWER IN GUACAMOLE

1 large cauliflower

Guacamole:
2 avocados
1 medium tomato, chopped
  fine

1 medium onion, chopped
  fine
La Victoria Green Taco Sauce
Salt
Chinese parsley (cilantro) *or*
  mint, *or* orégano

Method: In a large lidded pan, heat water to boiling, add cauliflower stem side down, cover and cook until tender (15-20 min.). Drain thoroughly, upside down. *Guacamole:* Peel, seed, and crush avocados with a fork, leaving some lumps. If not for immediate use, save a seed. To roughly mashed avocado pulp, add the tomato and onion. Add chile sauce cautiously, tasting until it meets your requirements, salt to taste, add the herbal seasoning you prefer, again to taste. If not to be used at once, put a seed in the middle of the guacamole—the Mexican preventative of discoloration; and squeeze some lemon juice over it. Cover tightly and refrigerate until needed. For this recipe the cauliflower is served hot with room temperature or cold guacamole, as a vegetable; both may be served cold as salad. Arrange cauliflower in center of a platter, surrounded by lettuce leaves; ice with guacamole, heavily. Sprinkle a handful of ruby-red pomegranate seeds over the whole to enhance the effect, especially if it is for a fall holiday. Time: 35 minutes. Serves 8.

NEAPOLITAN SNOW PUDDING

2 c. milk
1/2 stick cinnamon, slivered
1/3 c. sugar
3 T. blanched, well-ground
  almonds

6 egg whites
1 lemon rind, grated

Method: Boil milk with cinnamon and sugar for 10 minutes; add almonds and boil 5 more minutes. Stir to prevent sticking. Cool. To unbeaten egg whites, add the lemon rind and strained milk; stir all together well and bake in a buttered mold set in a pan of hot water in 350° until firm when shaken and beginning to be golden on top. (45 min.) Chill before serving. Total time, about 1 hour. Serves 6. Serve with Pudding Sauce

PUDDING SAUCE

2 c. water	6 yolks
2 c. sugar	1 c. orange juice

Method: Make syrup by boiling the sugar and water together five minutes after reaching boiling point. Cool 15 minutes. Beat the yolks and orange juice together in mixer, add to the syrup, and cook again on medium heat stirring constantly until mixture coats the spoon—approx. 15 minutes. To serve, have pudding and sauce well chilled. Run a thin knife around pudding to loosen it, and invert on a large platter. Pour the sauce over and around it. You may prefer to reduce the sugar for the sauce to 1-3/4, 1-1/2, or even 1 cup instead of 2—it is a *very* sweet syrup! If this reduction is made, it must be given more cooking time before it becomes syrupy. Time: 35 min. Serves 6.

Menu 21

CREAM OF CORN SOUP

4 egg yolks
1 qt. milk
4 T. cornstarch dissolved in
1/4 c. cold water
4 T. butter (optional)
2 c. tender young cooked corn
or 1 can cream style

2 canned green chiles
(Ortega)
1 t. salt
1/4 t. black pepper
1/4 to 1/2 t. fresh ground
nutmeg

Method: Beat yolks into milk in double boiler top over boiling water. Stir often. Blenderize corn and chiles, and add to milk and egg. Add cornstarch. Stir until mixture coats the spoon, in 5 to 7 minutes. Do not overcook or it will separate. Pass through sieve to remove unwanted particles, return to pot, add salt, butter, pepper and nutmeg. When again hot, serve with croutons. Time: 15-20 minutes. Serves 8.

ENCHILADAS VERDES

1 head iceberg lettuce
1 large onion
2 green onions
3/4 c. grated dry white cheese
2 bottles La Victoria Green
Taco Sauce

1 c. cream
1 egg
1 t. salt
1-1/2 c. cooking oil
24 tortillas

Method: On a large platter arrange half the lettuce, coarsely sliced. Slice large onion, soak in salt water 1/2 hour. Drain, dry with paper towels and separate into rings. Finely chop green onions and mix with large onion in bowl. Place cheese in another

65

bowl. Mix taco sauce, cream, egg and salt and warm, but not to point of cooking the egg. In a large pan heat the cooking oil (about 1/ 2 inch at a time). Quickly fry as many tortillas as the pan will hold, dipping them first into egg sauce, sliding them into pan and turning them over in the same order of putting them in—they should be limp, not crisp. When the last is turned, remove the first and dip into warm sauce, being sure both sides are coated. Place on paper plate, sprinkle with cheese and onion, fold, slide onto lettuce and continue with second tortilla. If you add a tortilla to the pan each time you take one out, and turn them also as you take out, you run less risk of getting them toasted. Don't let oil run out, nor drain it; they have to be a little greasy to be good. When they cover the lettuce, sprinkle all with cheese and onion and lettuce; then start the second layer on top of them. If any chile mixture remains, pour it over the last enchiladas before sprinkling with all remaining onion, cheese, and lettuce. Serve at once. Time without soaking of onion: about 45 minutes, the first time; with practice, 25-30. Serves 6-12.

PORK CHOPS GRILLED A LA YUCATAN

6 pork chops
Sour orange juice to cover, or
   orange and lemon juice
   mixed, or grapefruit juice
1/2 t. pepper
2 cloves garlic crushed with
   1 t. salt

Cooking oil for frying
1 pkg. frozen peas, boiled
2 T. butter
6 sprigs parsley, finely
   minced

Method: Soak chops in fruit juice, pepper, and garlic salt. Be sure meat is completely covered. Soak two hours (or more). Cook and drain peas. Preheat oven to 450°. Drain chops and dry with paper towels, brush with lard or oil, and broil ten minutes on each side, about four inches from broiler, until done. Fry peas in the butter. Remove chops to serving dish, arrange peas around them, and sprinkle with the parsley. Time (without marinade time): 20 minutes. Serves 6.

FRIJOLES WITH TORTILLAS

Used canned Rosarita Refried Beans, or see Menu 3 for recipe. Serve with fresh hot tortillas; or as a side dish with the enchiladas.

APRICOT CREAM

1 can apricot halves, or 2 c.
fresh fruit, peeled and
seeded
1 c. whipping cream

1/2 c. apricot liquid from can
1/2 c. sugar (if you use fresh
apricots, increse sugar to
3/4 c., cream to 1-1/2 c.

Method: Chop fruit fine, but leave some lumps. Whip the cream and combine with the fruit, liquid, and sugar. Pour into freezer pans and set in freezer. Ready in 2-3 hours. Makes 2 icecube trays full. Serves 8-12.

Menu 22

Potato-Ball Soup   Mountain Turkey
Cabbage with Cream   Almond Vanilla Pudding
Coffee

POTATO-BALL SOUP

Potato-Balls
1/4 lb. potatoes
1/2 t. grated nutmeg
2 T. butter
1 egg
4 T. butter

Soup
1 medium onion, minced
2 T. butter
1 medium tomato, well-
   chopped
1 chile verde, chopped
1/4 t. nutmeg
4 hard-boiled egg yolks,
   mashed
4 to 6 c. hot meat or chicken
   broth, or consommé

Method: Boil, peel and mash the potatoes. Mix with nutmeg, 2 T. butter, and egg. Between two spoons, shape into about 18 balls the size of a walnut, and fry in 4 T. butter until brown. Keep them warm. *Soup:* In remaining butter, fry the onion until transparent; add tomato, chile verde, nutmeg and yolks, and simmer until the tomato is cooked, about 15 minutes. Add to the hot broth. Add potato balls and serve at once. Time: 1 hr. Serves 6-8.

MOUNTAIN TURKEY

This recipe from Yucatan, calling for boiled turkey, is very good and worth trying. You may prefer to use turkey parts, such as two drumsticks and a breast. This recipe is for half a large turkey, or a whole small one. To adapt for turkey parts, use half the other ingredients. To facilitate eating, debone the turkey after it is cooked. However, the recipe does not demand deboning, which usually takes a good half hour as it must be done carefully. As the chops take less time, debone them anyway, and cut the meat into bite sizes.

1/2 large turkey, or 1 small
  turkey
6 pork chops
2 cloves garlic, crushed with
  1 t. salt
1/2 t. pepper

1/2 t. orégano, rubbed
  between palms
4 c. Masa Harina
2 t. salt
8-10 c. turkey broth
1/2 lb. butter

Method: Place the turkey and pork in your largest cooking pot, or perhaps your roaster. Add water to cover. Add the garlic, pepper, and orégano. Bring to a rapid boil, reduce heat, cover and cook until turkey is tender (2 hrs.) Keep the meat covered with water throughout cooking; if you need to add water, be sure it is hot. Remove turkey and meat and keep them hot. Measure the remaining broth. Return ten cupsful to the pot. In a bowl moisten the Masa Harina with 4 c. of cold water. Corn-meal, wet thoroughly with cold water, will not lump when added to boiling water. Bring broth again to a boil, empty the Masa Harina, salt, and butter into it, and stir and stir. Taste to correct seasoning. When it becomes *very* thick, empty half onto a large platter. Distribute the turkey over it, and the pork over the turkey. Empty the rest of the cornmean over the first layers. Let set 5 minutes before serving, partly to firm it, mainly to prevent anguished howls—hot cornmeal is very, very hot!

CABBAGE WITH CREAM

1 medium to large cabbage,
   cut into wedges
Salted water to cover
1 c. cream, sweet or sour, as
   preferred

1/2 t. pepper
1/2 t. nutmeg fresh grated
4 T. butter (1/2 cube)

Method: Cut cabbage into quarters, then cut into strips. Bring salted water to a rapid boil in a large saucepan. Drop in cabbage, cover, and boil fast until tender, 6 to 10 minutes. Drain thoroughly. Add cream (room temperature), pepper, nutmeg, and butter. Rapidly heat through. Taste to correct seasoning. The nutmeg should be plainly perceptible. Serve at once. Time: 15 min. One medium cabbage serves 4.

ALMOND VANILLA PUDDING

3 pints milk, scalded
   (or use evaporated)
3 yolks
1/2 c. blanched almonds

1 c. sugar
2 t. vanilla
1 pkg. gelatine dissolved in
   1/2 c. cold water

Method: Place milk, yolks, almonds, sugar and vanilla in top of double boiler over hot water until mixture coats spoon, stirring occasionally. Dissolve gelatine in cold water and set in small pan of hot water until it becomes transparent; stir into the other mixture and cool. Chill before serving. Time: 1/2 hour. Serves 6-8.

Sopa de Tortilla
Calabacitas

Red Snapper a la Veracruz
Adelita's Merengado

SOPA DE TORTILLA

1 dozen tortillas
1/2 c. cooking oil
1 large onion, minced
Garlic if desired, finely
    minced, or use 1/4 t. garlic
    salt
1 large tomato, peeled and
    crushed

1/4 t. orégano, *or* 1 t. finely
    chopped fresh mint, *or* 1 t.
    chile powder
1 t. salt
1/4 c. grated dry white cheese,
    Romano and/or Parmesan
2 hard-boiled egg yolks
1-2 T. butter

Method: Cut tortillas in fourths, and fry in hot cooking oil over medium heat only long enough to turn them golden. Remove them and keep them hot. In the same oil used for frying tortillas, fry onion and garlic until limp, add tomato, orégano, mint or chile and salt. In well-greased double boiler top, layer tortillas alternately with sauce and dry cheese; finish with sauce and cheese. On top put a garnish of egg yolks pressed through a sieve, and dot the whole with butter. Cover. Cook over boiling water 30 minutes. Time: 1 hour, 8 min. Serves 4-6.

RED SNAPPER A LA VERACRUZ

1 attractive red snapper 4 lbs.
Salt, flour, cooking oil
1 clove garlic, minced
1 t. salt
2 large onions, chopped
2 T. parsley, minced

4 large canned or fresh
    tomatoes
1 bay leaf
2 slices lemon
1/2 c. stuffed olives (4 oz.)
1/4 t. pepper

Method: Be sure all the scales are removed from fish; wipe it gently inside and out with a damp cloth. Dry. Score sides of fish three or four times with a sharp knife. Salt and flour the fish. Heat sufficient cooking oil (about 1/2 inch in a large pan, olive oil preferred) and then fry the fish over medium heat, first on one side then the other, until golden brown. (About five min. to each side.) The fish will be half-cooked. Transfer it to a well-greased baking pan or roaster, and cover to keep warm. Make sauce: Pour off excess oil from pan in which fish fried, leaving about 1/8 cupful. Reheat, and fry the garlic, salt and onion until the onion is golden. Add tomatoes, parsley, bay leaf, lemon, olives, and pepper. Bring to a rapid boil; reduce heat and simmer 10 to 15 minutes, crushing tomatoes with a spoon. Pour sauce over fish, and set the pan over low heat to season and simmer another 10 or 15 minutes; or place in 350° oven for the same length of time. Time: 45 min. Serves 8-10.

CALABACITAS

6-8 zucchini　　　　　　　1/2 t. salt
3 T. butter　　　　　　　　1/4 t. pepper
1 medium onion, minced　　1/4 t. orégano, if desired
1 tomato, peeled and crushed

Method: Wash but do not peel zucchini. In a large pan over medium heat, melt the butter, add the onions, cover, and simmer until onion is transparent, 3-5 minutes. Remove stems from zucchini and rapidly slice or cube zucchini into the pan. Add tomato, salt, pepper and orégano. If the tomato is very dry, add 1/4 c. hot water. Cover and cook 20-30 minutes, until zucchini is tender. Time: 35 minutes. Serves 6.

ADELITA'S MERENGADO

4 c. milk
1 c. sugar
1 stick cinnamon, crushed
Rind of 1 lemon, grated

4 egg whites
1 t. anise flavoring
1/4 c. sugar

Method: Combine milk, 1 c. sugar, cinnamon and lemon rind in large sauce pan, and bring rapidly to a boil. Lower heat and simmer 5 minutes. Strain. Cool. Beat the egg whites until stiff, then add the 1/4 c. sugar, very slowly, still beating. Add anise flavor to the milk, and carefully fold in the whites, avoiding breaking them up. Freeze several hours until set. This is a refreshing and delightful summer sherbet. In addition to the anise flavoring, you may add a teaspoonful of almond flavoring. In summer leave this snowy looking dessert coolly ungarnished, or decorate it only with a cool green leaf or two: mint, nasturtium, or lemon verbena. In winter try a sprinkle—very light— of instant cocoa, a dash of cinnamon, or a whisper of instant coffee. Time, including freezing time: 2-1/2 to 3 hours. Serves 6.

Menu 24

Wine Soup
Tongue with Banana

Macaroni with Spinach
Papaya and Orange Dessert

WINE SOUP

2 T. olive oil or butter
1 small onion, finely minced
2 T. flour
1 medium tomato, peeled
  and chopped
5 c. chicken or meat broth,
  heated

3 hard-boiled eggs, quartered
2 t. salt
1/2 t. pepper
2 slices bread
2 T. butter
1 c. red wine or claret

Method: Heat oil or butter, add onion and fry over medium heat until golden. Blend in flour until smooth, then add tomato. Cover tightly and simmer 10 min. Add tomato mix to heated broth; reduce heat and simmer ten minutes more. Add salt and pepper; taste to correct seasoning. Cut bread into cubes. Heat the butter, and fry the bread, stirring, until it has browned nicely. About 3 min. for two slices. Add the fried bread, the eggs and wine to the soup and serve at once. Time: 25 min. Serves 8.

MACARONI WITH SPINACH

3 T. cooking oil
1 lb. macaroni
2 T. cooking oil
1 large onion, minced
1 clove garlic, finely minced
2 medium tomatoes,
  finely chopped

1 pkg. frozen spinach, or
  1 bunch fresh spinach,
  boiled 3 min.
4 c. chicken or meat broth or
  consommé
2 t. salt, 1/2 t. pepper
1/2 c. grated dry white cheese
  (Romano, Parmesan, or
  both)

Method: In large deep pan, heat cooking oil. Break macaroni into two-inch pieces and fry in the oil until golden brown. Drain. In the same pan heat the 2 T. of cooking oil, add onion and garlic and fry until golden. Add tomato, reduce heat and simmer, crushing tomato as it cooks. When sauce thickens (about 10 min.) add the spinach, cooked, drained and chopped; then the macaroni. Barely cover with boiling water or stock, add salt and pepper, cover and reduce heat. Simmer until liquid is absorbed —about 25 min. Remove to large platter, sprinkle heavily with cheese, and serve. Total time: 45 minutes. Serves 12.

TONGUE WITH BANANA

1 tongue, boiled and peeled (2-1/2 to 3 lbs.)	1 T. vinegar
	4 T. cooking oil
1 large brown onion	2 T. raisins
2 large tomatoes	1 T. capers
1/2 t. cinnamon	3 half-ripe bananas, peeled,
1/4 t. cloves	each in four chunks
1 t. salt	3-4 sprigs parsley
1/4 t. orégano	

Method: Boil tongue until tender, usually 1-1/2 to 2 hours—once in a while one is tough and takes much longer. It is ready when a fork goes easily into it. Reserve liquid for other recipes. Let tongue cool, to handle easily. Slit outside skin down the center lengthwise underneath the tongue. Now with small sharp knife peel off all outer membrane—it should come off easily as a glove. Remove excess fat, gristle, bones. Slice tongue and keep it warm. In blender buzz onion, peeled and quartered, tomatoes, cinnamon, cloves, salt, orégano and vinegar. Heat oil and pour the tomato mixture into it. Simmer ten minutes. Add the raisins, capers, tongue and bananas. Cover tightly, and simmer ten minutes more. Serve on a large platter with minced parsley sprinkled over it, and parsley sprigs surrounding it. Time, after boiling tongue: 25 minutes. Serves 8.

PAPAYA AND ORANGE DESSERT

2 papayas   4 large oranges

Method: Make this 3 or 4 hours before serving. Cut papaya in half lengthwise, discard seeds, peel papaya and cut into neat cubes. Peel oranges, remove as much white membrane as possible, segment and remove remaining membrane and seeds, divide orange into bite sizes and stir into the papaya cubes. When oranges are properly sweet, nothing more is needed. If acid, dribble some honey over the fruit or sprinkle with sugar. Refrigerate. Serve in pretty glass cups or bowls, and enjoy. Preparation time: 10-15 min. Serves 8.

Menu 25

Poor Man's Soup   Breaded Ox-Tails
String Beans in Egg Sauce   Capuchinas
                    Coffee

POOR MAN'S SOUP

6 slices dried bread
1/2 c. olive oil
1 T. cooking oil
1 medium onion, minced
1 clove garlic, minced
1 c. chile sauce, red or green

1-1/2 c. milk
1/2 c. soft cheese, white,
    Provolone, cottage, goat
    cheese, Munster or Jack
Salt to taste

Method: Spread the bread slices out to dry an hour or two before
you begin. Cube bread slices. Heat olive oil and fry the cubes,
stirring constantly to prevent burning, until golden brown.
Remove to a bowl and keep them warm. In the same pan heat
the cooking oil and fry the onion and garlic until transparent.
Add chile sauce and milk, and bring quickly to a boil. Add the
cheese. Stir only until cheese begins to melt; then divide croutons
into small bowls and pour the soup over them. This is very rich—
hence the small bowls. The chile may be decreased to 1/2 cupful
or less, and milk increased to compensate. While either green or
red chile sauce may be used, I prefer the green. Time: about 20
min. Serves. 6.

BREADED OX-TAILS

1 ox-tail (ask your butcher
    to separate the segments,
    but leave the meat on each)
1 t. salt
1/2 t. ground cloves
1/4 t. cumin (ground)
1/4 t. pepper

1/4 t. marjoram
1/4 t. thyme
2 cloves of garlic, finely
    minced
1 c. vinegar
2 c. bread crumbs

Method: Allow one ox-tail to each three consumers (this recipe is exceptionally good!) and ask your butcher to separate the bones. The day before serving, grind the salt and all the spices and garlic together, then blend with the vinegar in a deep bowl and add the oxtails. Stir to make sure each piece is drenched and refrigerate; turn over with a spoon three times during next 24 hours. Empty all into a cooking pot, and add only such water as may be needed to cover the meat. Bring quickly to a boil, reduce heat, cover and simmer until tender. Remove and cool in its liquid. Drain. Add 1/4 t. salt and 1/4 t. pepper to crumbs and stir to mix well. Cut pieces of aluminum foil large enough for thorough wrapping of each piece of meat. Butter foil, and sprinkle with crumbs. In remaining crumbs, roll each piece of meat to coat well, lay each on a piece of foil, and wrap carefully. Under 400° broiler, broil each package about 15 min. on each side. Serve in foil. Good for either indoor or outdoor supper. While one ox-tail may serve six people, I would most certainly allow one to each three eaters unless all are weight-watchers! For each additional tail, multiply the marinade—double for two, triple for three, etc. Exclusive of soaking time: approx. 1 hour.

STRING BEANS IN EGG SAUCE

4 T. butter
4 sprigs parsley, finely
   minced
1 pkg. frozen French style
   string beans

1 egg yolk
1/8 c. vinegar
1/2 t. salt or sugar

Method: Melt butter, add parsley (discard stems). Sauté over medium heat until parsley wilts, about 3 min. Add frozen beans, cover, and sauté over slow heat. Stir once or twice to speed deicing. When beans are tender (20 min.) beat yolk into vinegar, add to beans, stir well, and stir and cook until yolk is set—but no longer. About 5 min. Taste, and if necessary, season with salt or sugar. Time: 30 min. Serves 4.

CAPUCHINAS

1/2 c. sugar for caramelizing   1 c. sugar
12 egg yolks   1 c. water
1 egg white

Method: Beat the 11 yolks and 1 whole egg together for 15 min. in your mixer, until very thick. Caramelize the sugar and spread it in the bottom of a buttered mold. I use a round ceramic ovenware bowl that is 8" in diameter and 3-1/2" deep. Theoretically it needs no greasing, but buttering the mold helps the custard slip from it more easily. Boil the sugar and water together five minutes and cool. Still beating the eggs, pour the cooled syrup slowly into them. Pour into the mold, set it in a pan of hot water, and bake uncovered in a 350° oven for about an hour, until firm. Cool and run a spatula around the rim of the custard. Turn out on a large pretty round glass dish. Be sure it is *cold* before you turn it out, or the custard will break. Be sure platter or dish is not too flat; the caramelized sugar becomes a plentiful sauce. Time: 1 hour 20 min. Serves 10 meagerly, 6-8 generously.

Menu 26

Tomato Soup   Green Chile Turnovers
Marinated Fish   Pineapple Rice Pudding

TOMATO SOUP

6 large ripe tomatoes, *or*
  1 # 2-1/2 can tomatoes
1/2 lb. chopped ham, raw
4 c. chicken or beef broth

1 pkg. frozen young peas, *or*
  1 small can French peas
Salt, pepper, to taste

Method: Boil tomatoes until tender in the least possible amount of water; or use canned. Press through sieve to remove skin and seed, or buzz in blender. Fry ham, which should have some fat, until well browned. Combine tomatoes with broth in a large pot, add ham, bring to a boil. Reduce heat. Simmer 15 min. During the simmering add peas, and salt and pepper to taste. Total time: 30 min. Serves 6.

GREEN CHILE TURNOVERS

Masa Harina, 2 C.
Cheese, dry white grated, 1/4 c.
Salt, 1/2 t.
Cooking oil, 2 T.
Boiling water, 1-1/2 c.

Jack cheese, strips 1/2 in. wide
  and abt. 1/4 inch thick
Green chiles, Ortega, 3-4,
  each in 4 strips
Oil for cooking

Method: Mix Masa Harina, dry cheese and salt; add cooking oil and water to make a thick but spreadable dough. Divide into 12-16 portions, shape into balls, and press each between two pieces of waxed paper with a flat board, applying even pressure. On each tortilla, place a strip each of cheese and chile, and using bottom piece of waxed paper to help, fold over the tortilla, press edges together. In a large pan heat 1/4 inch of cooking oil and fry the turnovers until golden brown on each side. Serve at once with a sauce of 1/2 c. sour cream and 1/2 c. green taco sauce, blended. Time: 45 min. Makes 12 fair-sized, or 16 daintier, turnovers.

MARINATED FISH

2 lbs. good white fish, boned,
   fileted
1 large onion, thinly sliced
2 long canned green chiles
   (Ortega)
4-6 small dried red peppers
2 buds of garlic

1 t. salt
20 to 40 small wild or bitter
   oranges—they yield very
   little juice, so 1 grapefruit
   and lemon or limes may be
   used instead

Method: In large pan heat water to boiling, gently add fish fillets; reduce heat but keep bubbling for 15 minutes. Slice onions and separate rings. Juice oranges; and in a small pan simmer the red peppers in just enough water to cover. Drain filets and discard water. Blenderize the red chiles and the water in which they cooked with the garlic and salt. In a large bowl with cover, alternate layers of fish slices, sliced or minced green chile, and red chile mixture, until all the filets are used. Strain the fruit juice over all, or remove the seeds and leave the fruit particles. Make sure fish is totally covered. Refrigerate 24 hours before serving. To serve, drain off sauce and arrange fish attractively on lettuce leaves. This is always served cold; it makes a pleasing dish. Without soaking time: 20 minutes. Serves 8-10.

PINEAPPLE RICE PUDDING

3 c. water
1 c. rice
1 13-oz. can evaporated milk
1 c. sugar

1 small can crushed pine-
   apple, drained
1 t. vanilla or almond extract
2 t. cinnamon

Method: Bring water to a rapid boil, add rice, cover pot and reduce heat to minimum. When the water is absorbed and rice tender (25 min.), drain. Add all the other ingredients to the rice and stir well. Chill thoroughly. If you prefer it less sweet, 1/2 cup sugar suits most American tastes. This pudding may be turned into an oiled mold to cool. Time: 30 min. Serves 8.

Menu 27

Zucchini-Tomato Soup | Rice Stew
Sweetbreads with Chile Sauce | Sherried Oranges

ZUCCHINI-TOMATO SOUP

4 to 8 tender zucchini   1 T. onion flakes
  (6 to 7 inches)   2 cans tomato soup
Water to cover   1/4 t. pepper
2 T. butter   Oyster crackers or croutons

Method: Boil zucchini until tender in water to cover in a 3-4 qt. pot, about 10 min. Remove zucchini, and crush roughly. Return to water in pot (there should be about 4 cups). Add soup and stir thoroughly. Heat butter and sauté onion flakes until golden. Add with pepper to the soup. When it boils again, serve. This is very good with oyster crackers or croutons. Time: 25 min. Serves 8.

RICE STEW

3 c. chicken broth   1 link chorizo, peeled and
1 c. rice   sliced, or Polish Kohlbase,
1/2 c. cooked ham, cubed   or 1/2 c. home-made chorizo
                    Salt (only if needed)

Method: Heat chicken broth to boiling, add rice, and half of the ham and the chorizo. Reduce heat, cover tightly, and simmer 20 min. or until rice is tender. Taste, and add salt if needed. Grease a casserole. Place half the rice in it, the rest of the meats mixed together, and cover with remaining rice. Cover and bake 30 min. at 350°. Time: 55 min. Serves 6.

SWEETBREADS WITH CHILE SAUCE

2 lbs. sweetbreads
Salt, pepper

1/4 c. olive oil or butter
1/2 to 1 c. green chile sauce

Method: Soak the sweetbreads for an hour in fresh salted water. Drain. Drop them in boiling water, reduce heat and boil gently 5 minutes. Remove and drain. Dry with paper towels. Cut sweetbreads in cubes and sprinkle lightly with salt and pepper (use shakers). Heat the oil or butter, and sauté sweetbreads until golden; add chile sauce and simmer until the sauce begins to bubble. Omitting soaking time: approx. 20 minutes. Serves 6 adequately, four generously. These are easy and delicious.

SHERRIED ORANGES

6 large sweet oranges
1/2 c. sugar
1/4 c. sweet sherry

Large whole strawberries for garnish

Method: Peel oranges, carefully removing all the white membrane possible. With a very sharp knife, slice oranges about 1/2 inch thick. If not seedless, remove all seeds. Arrange on your best glass platter, sprinkle with sugar and sherry. Refrigerate at least three hours before serving—but not so long that they begin to wilt. Decorate with the strawberries, also chilled. If you have access to a few young orange leaves, or leaves and blossoms, unsprayed, these make a fine garnish; so do a few sprigs of lovely fresh green mint leaves. This is an admirable spring and summer dessert; and is also good in winter for balancing heavy winter meals. Time (without refrigeration): about 15 min. Serves 6 to 8.

Menu 28

Pigs' Feet in Escabeche   Boiled Potatoes
Onions Sliced in Vinegar   Pickled Chiles
Tortillas or French Bread   Fruit Surprise

PIGS' FEET IN ESCABECHE

Pigs' feet (as many as desired;   1/4 to 1/2 c. shortening
  allow 1 to each serving.)   2 c. red or white wine, dry
2 bay leaves   1/4 c. vinegar
2 carrots   1 T. sugar
1 t. salt   1 t. cinnamon
1 egg for each 2 feet   1/2 t. ground cloves
1 t. flour for each egg   2 T. toasted sesame seeds
1/2 t. salt

Method: Cook the pigs' feet in water with bay leaves, carrots, and 1 t. salt, until tender (2 hrs.) Remove from water, cool, and discard all bones. Toast sesame seed in small pan over heat, stirring. Pin together pieces of pigs' feet with toothpicks, to be removed before serving. Make chunks about 2" x 2". Beat egg whites until stiff, add yolks slowly, one at a time; still beating slowly add flour. Season with salt. Dip chunks in this batter, and fry until golden on all sides in the heated oil (about 1/2 inch deep in pan). Remove from pan. There should be about 2 tablespoonsful of oil left; if it looks like less, add some. Add wine, vinegar, sugar and spices to this fat. Bring to boil, return pigs' feet to pan, reduce heat, cover pan. Simmer five minutes. Sprinkle with toasted sesame seed and serve at once. Time: 3 hrs. 35 min. Serves 8.

BOILED POTATOES (Mexican style)

Peel even, regular-sized potatoes. Place in saucepan with a well-fitting lid with 1 t. salt and 1/2 c. water. Cover pan tightly. Bring water to a boil; reduce heat and continue cooking until potatoes are thoroughly done, shaking the pan occasionally to prevent sticking. This takes about half an hour—it depends on size of the potatoes. Serve with plenty of butter and pepper.

ONIONS IN VINEGAR

Select large Bermuda or red onions. Peel and slice as thinly as possible. Use a bowl with tight-fitting lid, and cover the onions with equal parts of water and vinegar, 1 t. salt, 1/2 t. Orégano, and a good pinch of pepper, at least 1/2 teaspoonful. Lift and stir to separate rings and distribute marinade evenly. (15-20 min.) Cover, and place in refrigerator for at least six hours before serving. Drain well. Save the vinegar to use in salad dressings or to pour over meat as a tenderizer. These keep a long time.

PICKLED CHILES

Many stores carry these. If there is neither a Mexican section in your supermarket nor Mexican grocery near you, try an Italian grocery—their pickled chiles are milder than Mexican chiles, anyway. At a Mexican grocery, ask for "Fruta en Vinagre." (Pickled Fruits). In addition to chiles, this contains fruits and other vegetables and is delicious. To make your own: Pack chiles in a sterilized quart jar, preferably green chiles, long and thin or small and plump. Fill jar 3/4 full of vinegar and finish filling with water; add a tablespoonful of salt, and a generous pinch of orégano. Make lid tight, and ripen a few weeks in any cook place —the vinegar preserves the chiles so refrigeration is not mandatory. If you wish, stab the chiles through and through with a large needle before pickling.

FRUIT SURPRISE

Crema de Leche:

2 T. cornstarch

1/2 c. sugar

2 c. milk

2 eggs

2 T. vanilla

12-18 large lady fingers, *or* sponge cake slices

1 box strawberries

2-6 ripe bananas

Method: Make *Crema de Leche* first: Mix sugar and cornstarch together in a small bowl. Combine milk and eggs in a quart sauce-pan, bring quickly to boiling point, then add the sugar and cornstarch, and stir over medium heat until the mixture coats the spoon, about 5 minutes. Cool. Stir in vanilla. This alone, served well-chilled, is a quick and easy Mexican dessert. But sometimes we want to be a little fancier, and then a pretty bowl is lined with lady fingers, vanilla wafers, or cake slices; then hulled strawberries and peeled ripe bananas, sliced, are added. Pour the cooled *crema de leche* over it all. Chill for at least 2 hours. Time (not counting refrigeration): 25 minutes. Serves 8.

Menu 29

Baked Tacos   Tripe with Chorizo and Garbanzos
Pears in Wine   Coffee

BAKED TACOS

12 tortillas
3 T. cooking oil
1 lb. Munster, Jack,
   Monterey or panela cheese

1 4-oz. can green chiles
1 c. sour cream

Method: Grease baking dish. Preheat oven to 350°. Heat short-ening over medium flame. Slice 12 strips of cheese. Slice four chiles into 3 strips each, or six chiles into 2 strips each. Dip each tortilla in hot oil, place on paper plate, put a strip of cheese and a strip of chile in it, roll up and place in baking dish. When first layer is finished, sprinkle lightly with salt and make second layer on top, salt, etc. Bake 15 min. Serve with or without sour cream on each taco. I like the contrast of the cold cream with hot taco. You may, if you wish, ladle the cream over the tacos and bake it with them. It's excellent either way. Time: 30 min. Serves 4-6.

TRIPE WITH CHORIZO AND GARBANZOS

1 to 2 lb. tripe
Lemon juice or vinegar
1 veal knuckle
1 c. ham bits or 2 ham hocks
2 links chorizo, peeled
2 cans garbanzo (chick-peas)
2 cloves of garlic crushed
   with 1 t. salt
1 green bell pepper, deveined,
   seeded, sliced; or 1 can
   chiles verdes sliced

3 cloves of garlic
1/2 t. salt
1/8 t. cumin seed, ground
A pinch of saffron
8 coriander seeds, ground
1 slice of French bread, about
   2 inches thick, soaked in
   1 c. broth with 1/4 c.
vinegar

Method: Wash tripe in hot water, rub with lemon juice of vinegar. Place to boil in a five quart saucepan, with veal knuckle, ham, chorizo, garbanzo with its liquid, lemon juice, garlic salt, and peppers; add water to cover. Boil for 1/2 hour. Extract tripe and cut into one inch squares, return to pot and continue simmering 1 to 1-1/2 hours longer, until tender. Grind the additional garlic and salt with the cumin, coriander, and peppercorns. Add to pot. Soak the bread in a cupful of the broth from pot with the vinegar, then blenderize and add to pot. (Add a little additional hot water if needed.) Simmer an additional 15 minutes. Serve with lemon wedges, coarsely chopped lettuce, finely sliced green onions, and chile sauce, each in its own bowl. Time: 2 hrs. 15 min. Serves 10.

PEARS IN WINE

4 to 6 large ripe firm pears
Water to cover, with juice of
  1 lemon
3/4 c. white port wine
1/2 c. water
1/2 c. sugar

1 T. lemon juice plus
  grated rind of 1 lemon
Fruit preserves (optional)
  abt. 1/2 c.
4 whole cloves
2 t. cornstarch, dissolved
  in 1/4 c. water

Method: Peel fruit, cut in halves lengthwise, and remove cores. Drop in water with the lemon juice as peeled to prevent discoloration. Combine in quart saucepan 1/2 c. water, the wine, sugar, lemon rind, and cloves, and bring to boil. Drop pears (drained) in the syrup, reduce heat and simmer until tender (15 min.). Cool. Remove fruit to attractive serving dish. If desired, fill halves with pineapple, apricot or raspberry preserves or jam. Otherwise, place hollow side down. Dissolve cornstarch and add to the liquid in the pan, and boil rapidly, stirring, until the liquid becomes transparent (5 min.). Cool, and strain sauce over pears. Equally good made with ruby port. Total time (without chilling): 25 min. Serves 4-6.

Menu 30

TAMALADA

Tamales: Beef, Chicken, Pork and Sweet
Atole   Beer
Coffee

A *tamalada* is a party to which people are invited for the sole
purpose of eating and enjoying tamales with something to drink.
In Mexico the traditional "something" is *atole*, a corn gruel stem-
ming from the time of the Aztecs. Often beer and coffee are
served also. The beer is excellent with the savory tamales, the
coffee with the sweet. Atole is delicious; but the taste for it sometimes requires cultivation. A tamalada is an unusually enjoyable
party for young people or children, as it cannot be formal. Pro-
vide large platters or empty cartons for discarding the wrappings
of the tamales—and no fair keeping score on how many are
consumed!

HOW TO MAKE TAMALES

Start a day or two ahead! Buy ingredients and prepare fillings in
advance. Try to have a friend or two or three come over early to
help you—if you have an assembly line, it is fun and easy and
you finish fast, but if you do it all yourself you may be too tired to
enjoy the fun when serving time comes. It is a tedious and fatigu-
ing job to make tamales for a crowd of people. I speak from
experience, both ways. However, I've thought about it and have
decided that if I ever do tackle it alone again, I'll make one kind
of tamale and freeze it; then do unrelated things the next day,
and the third day make a batch of another kind, etc. They may
be frozen ready for cooking, or after being cooked. They keep
beautifully, and cook rapidly. So either method works out com-
fortably. Frozen cooked, an hour of steaming should completely
defrost and heat them all the way through. Frozen uncooked, I'd
be inclined to allow 1-1/2 hours. The traditional wrapping for
tamales is corn husks, in Mexico called Hojas, which simply
means leaves. Many grocery stores now have them in their Mexican departments, sold in large cellophane packages, each enough

for perhaps two tamaladas. Sometimes the label says *Husks*. Some have been handled so carefully that the only preparation needed is a soak in *hot hot* water; but some have corn silk, worm spots, perhaps a worm or two! (Dead. Harmless.) The best way is to plunge them into very hot water until cool enough to handle, placing a large platter over them to hold them down. The hojas become soft and pliable. Clean them of cornsilk, and scissor off wormy parts. Do this before helpers come, and leave husks in clean hot water until nearly time to use them. Dry between paper or dish towels in dozens as required—2 or 3 dozen each time. Husks broken or too narrow are torn lengthwise into "strings" (about 1/2 inch wide) for tying up the tamales. I confess that I now use twine. The hoja strings are traditional, but easily break while you work with them.

If husks are not obtainable, use aluminum foil cut in pieces about 8" x 10". In Yucatan and Colombia, they use banana leaves. Banana leaves, after cutting in sections, must be boiled briefly before using to make them pliable and prevent splitting. If you use any of these untraditional wrappings, tie them with string. Rubber bands are great, too! If you use waxed paper, use double thickness.

Method of making: Take a corn husk, or if small, two husks and overlap them, to form a shape about 6" x 8" across, and the normal length of the husk. Spread dough over it, leaving exposed about an inch from bottom and three inches from top. Place a slightly mounded tablespoonful of filling on the dough, including some of the liquid. Fold the right section of husk over the middle, and the left to slightly overlap the right; fold up the bottom. Bend the top down toward the middle, and securely tie the resulting package. In Mexico it is general practice to tie each variety in its own pattern for easy identification when serving. For instance, chicken tamales may have a string around each end; beef tamales only one string around the middle. Little sweet tamales almost invariably are made like little purses—the dough placed in the middle of the husk, right edge folded over, left edge folded over, and the top and bottom folded to meet at the top and there be gathered together and tied firmly like a bag pudding. Some space should be left for tamales to expand, which they do while steaming. Steaming time: 1 to 2 hours. When tamales are small and have dough very thinly spread, they may be done even before the hour is up. The thinly spread are the very best. But most of us are inexperienced, and a doughy tamal is not as good as one that has really firmed up, so to be on the safe side, give them 1-1/2 hours and then break one open to find out what is happening. If you make many, for 10 people of more— you need a large steamer.

Some cooks put a little baking powder in their tamal dough to make it lighter. Some use hot water instead of hot broth, in which case salt must be added, too. Hot broth usually is salted. After mixing the dough, cooks who are very particular about having tamales fine and light beat it for a long time—and here a mixer helps. I have made them often, sometimes well-beaten and sometimes just-thrown-together, and have not been able to detect any vast difference. At most tamal parties three kinds of meat-or-fowl tamales are usually served. Sweet ones are brought in last as dessert.

BEEF FILLING FOR TAMALES

1/4 c. cooking oil
1-1/2 lb. chopped or ground beef, or chuck or round cut in very small cubes
1 large onion, minced
2 large tomatoes, cubed
1 small bottle olives (any kind except ripe)
1 can green chiles, or chile powder—1-5 t., or 1 large red chile, deveined, seeded, and ground

10-15 sprigs parsley, minced
1/2 t. orégano, rubbed between palms
2 large carrots, cubed
1 large potato, peeled and cubed
3 zucchini, cubed—all 3 vegetables dice-sized
Garlic: (optional) 1-4 cloves
Fruta en vinagre: 5 or 6 pieces, if obtainable
Salt and pepper

Method: In a very large pan, in 1/4 c. cooking oil, over high heat, stir and fry beef and onions together until beef is browned, about 10 minutes. Reduce heat and add tomatoes, olives and their liquid, chopped chiles; the whole can makes what I call mildly hot tamales, but this only if you extract all seeds. If you use Gebhardt's chile powder, add one teaspoonful only, and after filling is cooked, if too bland, cautiously add teaspoon by teaspoon (dissolved in pan juices) stirring in and tasting until it suits you. Add parsley, orégano, carrots, potato and zucchini, all in small cubes, 1/4 to 1/2 inch wide . . . and garlic. Cover and cook until vegetables are well done and hash is not too juicy. I usually remove some of the liquid at the start of cooking and return it to pan after the volume goes down; I like to give it plenty of time for flavor to blend well; but an hour will serve if you lack time. The mix should be juicy otherwise tamales will be dry. The level of liquid should be slightly reduced below level of solids. Taste to correct seasoning. Don't worry if you can't find *fruta en vinagre,* but if you can, add four or five pieces, whole, as well as several tablespoonsful of their vinegar; they give the tamales a pleasant flavor, and four or five eaters a pleasant surprise! Time: 1 hour.

DOUGH FOR BEEF TAMALES

Recipe for Prepared Masa OR	*Recipe for Masa Harina*
6 c. prepared masa	3 c. Masa Harina
Water to soften slightly	1 c. shortening
2 c. shortening, lard preferred	3 c. boiling broth (beef
1 t. salt	preferred) or hot water
	1 t. salt

Method: Heat the shortening with the broth or water and salt, but not if you use prepared masa. Beat it into the Masa Harina. You may use the mixer. If you use prepared masa, work the shortening into it—make it easier by having it at room temperature—then add the salt and only enough hot water to make the masa spreadable. It should be like peanut butter at room temperature in summer. Time: 15 minutes. Makes 50-60 tamales.

FILLING FOR CHICKEN TAMALES

1 3 lb. chicken
1 bay leaf
1 t. salt
1/4 c. cooking oil
1 large onion, minced
1 # 2-1/2 can tomatoes
10-15 sprigs parsley
Pinch of saffron
1/4 t. orégano
1/4 c. raisins
1/2 c. blanched almonds
3 carrots cubed small

3 zucchini cubed small
1 or 2 small pickled green
   chiles (optional; but they
   do make the tamales taste
   good!)
1 small bottle green olives,
   any kind, or 1/2 c.
1/2 t. cumin seed, ground
1/2 t. coriander seed, ground
Additional chile powder or
   chiles as desired

Method: Put chicken to cook in a large pot with water to cover, bay leaf and salt. Boil until well done, about 45 min. In Mexico the bones are left in it. I remove them; it makes eating the tamales easier and less messy to handle. Deboning chicken usually takes from 20 min. to 1/2 hour. Reserve the chicken broth for the tamale dough. While chicken boils, in a very large pan heat 1/4 c. cooking oil, fry the onion until golden (3 min.); add the tomatoes, well-crushed, the parsley (stems discarded, leaves minced), saffron, orégano, raisins, blanched almonds, carrots, zucchini, salt. Most spices are better ground when needed. If you use the little pickled chiles, even though whole, this may be seasoned enough for you, although it's almost a certainty it will need more salt. Tomatoes are great salt-consumers and so is cornmeal. In fact, I find it better to have all my tamal fillings taste a little *over*-seasoned, so much of the flavor seems to diminish during cooking . . . or when teamed with the cornmeal. Simmer the mixture 10 minutes, then taste. If too bland, add moistened chile powder until it suits. A good combination is about 1/2 t. red hot New Mexican or Cayenne chile with a tablespoonful or two of bland paprika. Simmer uncovered until all the vegetables are tender and mixture well thickened, about 25 min. more. Makes 50-60 tamales. Time: 1 hour.

DOUGH FOR CHICKEN TAMALES

4 c. Masa Harina
3 c. chicken broth, boiling
1 c. lard

1 t. salt (unless broth is
salted)

Method: Mix together and beat well. Makes 50-60 tamales.

FILLING FOR PORK TAMALES

2 lbs. pork spare-ribs, farmer
style (have butcher sepa-
rate them and cut into 2
inch lengths)

1 t. salt
1 bottle green taco sauce

Method: Boil spare-ribs in water to cover with 1 t. salt until tender. If desired, add one or two cloves of garlic. When well-done, drain spare-ribs and mix with taco sauce. It is not necessary to remove bones from the meat. Neither is it against the rules. Time: 1 hour. Makes 20-25 tamales.

DOUGH FOR PORK TAMALES

3 c. Masa Harina
2 c. pork broth, boiling

1 c. lard, room temperature
1 t. salt

Method: Mix together. Beat well. Time: 10 minutes. Makes 20-25.

SWEET TAMALES

4 c. Masa Harina
1 c. sugar
1 t. salt
3 inches stick cinnamon,
crushed
2 c. lard, room temperature

Boiling water to make soft
dough, about 4 c.
1 c. raisins
1 c. blanched almonds, whole
or halved
Red vegetable coloring

Method: Mix the Masa Harina, sugar, salt, cinnamon, and add the lard and boiling water; stir and beat until dough is soft but not runny. Add raisins and almonds and beat them in with a spoon. Cool for ease in handling. Just before putting dough into husks, stir in a few streaks of vegetable coloring—about 1/8 teaspoon—do not *mix* in, stir only a few times, to make dough streaky. Use about a soupspoonful of dough to each small tamale. Children love 'em. Use the smaller husks for wrapping. Warn eaters about the cinnamon—that it is edible. They may think the cook has been careless and let slivers of rubbish fall into the tamales and start picking them out—or they may reject the tamale altogether. Time: 20 minutes. Makes 40 tamales.

WARNING: While the fillings can only improve by being made a day or so before, the doughs never should be made more than an hour or two before cooking, and should be kept warm and spreadable.

ATOLE

Atole is made plain or salted, but far more often sweetened and flavored. It is served at booths in most of the market places in Mexico, as an early morning and late evening drink. Some of its many flavors: pineapple, strawberry, almond, vanilla, tamarind, blackberry, cinnamon. When chocolate is the flavor, it is no longer *atole:* that is *champurrado.* In our family we discovered that pineapple atole, thoroughly chilled, is a refreshing and delightful summer drink.

CINNAMON ATOLE

5 c. milk
1 stick cinnamon, finely slivered

1/2 c. Masa Harina
1/4 c. sugar
1 c. water

Method: Put milk and cinnamon in pot to boil over high heat. In a medium-sized mixing bowl, stir together the Masa Harina and sugar, add the water and stir until smooth. When milk boils, pour the Masa mixture *slowly* into the milk, so that boiling is not slowed, stirring all the while. Reduce heat slightly and continue stirring to prevent sticking. When mixture reaches the consistency of thin boiled custard—about 5 minutes—remove and cool about five minutes, then serve at once. If you wish, strain it. If you like it sweeter, add more sugar. Time: 15 min. Serves 8-10.

PINEAPPLE ATOLE

Instead of cinnamon, use 1 small can of crushed pineapple. Follow above recipe omitting cinnamon, but do not add pineapple until *after* the mixture has thickened and been removed from heat—it curdles if pineapple is added too soon.

STRAWBERRY ATOLE

Use 1 basket of strawberries, hulled, washed, crushed, and follow directions for pineapple atole.

CHAMPURRADO

Follow instructions for *Cinnamon Atole*, omitting cinnamon if you use Ibarra's Mexican Chocolate, which has its own cinnamon. If you do use it, melt it in about 1/2 cup of boiling water over low heat to add to the atole mixture. Use one whole cake. If you use American bitter chocolate, dissolve 3 squares in 1/2 c. boiling water; increase sugar to your own taste.

Don't forget, the best way, and most fun, to have a tamalada is to have four or five friends come about two hours early to help you. Allow plenty of time.

HASTA LUEGO
(Until We Meet Again)